C000145046

## Publisher's Note

❧❦ ❧❦ ❧❦ ❧❦ ❧❦ ❧❦ ❧❦ ❧❦

[Pg 1]

# Ancient Chinese Account of the Grand Canyon, or Course of the Colorado

(Copyrighted, Brooklyn, 1913)
By ALEXANDER M'ALLAN

## TEN SUNS IN THE SKY!

The ancient Chinese records tell of a "Place of Ten Suns," where "Ten Suns rose and shone together" (see Appendix, note 1).

Seven Suns were also seen shining together in the sky! and at night (if indeed we can call it "night") as many as seven moons! (What a haunt for lovers and poets!)

Five Suns were also beheld (see note 2).

What Liars those Chinese writers are!

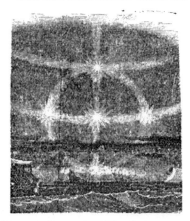

Figure 1. Spectacle of Five Suns.

Very good; but why not denounce all our own Arctic navigators as a pack of Liars? They all tell about more Suns than one! A picture of Five (see Figure 1) is furnished by a most eminent explorer (note 3). The dictionaries and cyclopedias of our careful publishers call the appearance of two or more suns (or moons) a **Parhelion**. The number of the multiplied "luminaries" never exceeds Ten (note 4). There actually is a "Place of Ten Suns."

Ten Suns say the Ancients.
Ten Suns say the Moderns.
[Pg 2]

## AMERICA SHAPED LIKE A TREE.

The ancient Mexicans likened North America to a Tree—a stupendous **Mulberry Tree**—"planted in the land known to us today as South America" (n. 5).

The Chinese geographers or mythologists teach that at a distance of 30,000 le (10,000 miles) to the east there is a land 10,000 le (over 3,000) miles in width.

Now the land referred to must be North America, for, 10,000 miles east from southern China brings us to California; and we further find that North America, now reached, is 10,000 le, or over 3,000 miles in width, measuring from the Pacific to the Atlantic.

The Chinese accounts further call our eastern realm a **Fu-Sang** (or Helpful Mulberry) land.

A **Mulberry** land (3,000 miles wide) is **There**, say the Chinese.

The **Mulberry** land (3,000 miles wide) is **Here**, say the Mexicans.

Like the Mexicans, the Chinese sages declare that there is an enormous Tree—the **Fu** (or helpful) **Sang Tree**—in the eastern Mulberry land 3,000 miles wide.

As just remarked, the Chinese call the enormous Eastern Tree a **Sang**, and the Mexicans call their enormous Tree a **Beb** (both terms standing for the **Mulberry**,—a fact to which no writer hitherto has directed, or called, attention.)

Observe (see Figure 2) that at Tehauntepec (a little west of Yucatan) our continent narrows down to a width of 100 miles (or 300 Chinese **le**).

The Mexicans say that North America is a Tree, and that it has a correspondingly enormous Trunk,—which at Tehauntepec measures 100 miles (or 300 Chinese **le**).

Now the Chinese writers declare that the enormous Mulberry in the region east of the Flowery Kingdom has "a Trunk of 300 **le**" (or 100 miles.) What a prodigious dimension! (see note 6.)

A Mulberry Tree, with a "Trunk of 300 **le**," is **There**, say the Chinese.

A Mulberry Tree, with a Trunk of 300 **le**, is **Here**, say the Mexicans.

Such a stupendous Tree ought to have enormous Branches to match the Trunk, and we are not surprised when informed that our monarch of the forest goes up—up—up even to the Place of the 10 Suns (in the Arctic zone.)

The One true sun is, of course, high

above the mountain ranges, or "Branches" of our Continental Mulberry.

But the extra Nine are false or delusive and mere reflections of the true sun on fog or vapor. The Chinese account, truly enough, states that they bear **wu**, and this term stands for "blackness," "inky," or "dark" (Williams dict. p. 1058.)

This identical term **wu** also stands for black or dark **fowls**, such as the raven, blackbird, and crow; and one Oriental scholar, dwelling indeed in Japan, assures us that each of the Nine Suns bears a **Crow**! We are seriously informed, that "all bear—literally cause to ride—a **Crow**" (note 7.)

As well might it be asserted that because **wu** signifies "black," the Nine **Wu** borne by the Suns must be nine blacks or negroes! The supposition that [Pg 3] Nine **Crows** are meant is absurd and contradicted by the luminaries themselves.

Figure 2. Our Continental American Tree. Strange to say, the "luminaries" emit no radiance! The light that is in them is darkness, and they are fitting symbols for commentators—black, white, yellow, and green—who have written learnedly and positively on them without understanding a thing about them. Perhaps it might be well, apart from its inconvenience, when writing about any nation, place, or natural object, to ascertain the position and name of the **continent** in which the subject of study is situated. Of course we are not so unreasonable as to insist that we must really comprehend a matter before getting up to explain it to others, but the positions of continents dealt with ought, as a rule, to be clearly ascertained. In the present instance we have faithfully followed the ancient directions and groped our way

into the presence of the Nine blind suns. Gazing at their beaming disks we perceive how the term wu (black or dark) applies to them. The **color** of Crows is there, but not the living birds themselves. It is the story of the Three Black Crows advanced another stage on its career of misrepresentation, and magnified Threefold. The Nine Suns have neither swallowed nor disgorged Nine Black Crows. But they are certainly open to the charge of having feasted too freely on diet no less dark and deceptive.

They're the **color** of Crows, say the Ancients.

They **bear** Nine Crows, say the Moderns.

[Pg 4]

The truth is that the false suns furnish neither heat nor light and really consist of dark (**wu**) vapor.

The Nine are mere reflections of the low-declined, true sun on "surrounding" frozen haze or mist, in extremely cold weather. When this icy fog seems—merely seems, of course,—to touch and surround the true sun, the illusions known as false suns are apt to appear. They obey some optical code of laws or signals understood best perhaps by themselves, and will sometimes disappear in a moment like a flock of timid "sun birds" (or wild geese—see note 8.) Their design apparently is to cheer and escort their illustrious sire in his otherwise lonesome trip through a frozen, desolate zone. Some Chinese accounts call them "children"—"children of the sun," etc., etc.

There is a reference to this frozen mist, in Verne's "Fur Country," reading as follows: "It is not a mist or fog,' he said to his companions, 'it is frost-rime,' a dense vapor which remains in a state of complete congelation. But whether a fog or a frozen mist, this phenomenon was none the less to be regretted for it rose a hundred feet at least above the level of the sea, and it was so opaque that the colonists could not see each other when only two or three paces apart."—Danvers' translation, p. 288.

It should be remarked that the frozen haze which breeds the false suns is

found only "at the bottom of," or "below," the mountain ranges or "branches" of our North American Mulberry Tree. The false suns speedily disappear from the view of the observer who climbs up out of the thick stratum of frozen fog or mist and ascends the nearest "Branch."

Such observations are completely in accord with the ancient Chinese declaration that Nine of the suns are to be seen "below" (**hia**) or "at the bottom of" the Branches, and One "above" the Branches. The suns (see note 9) are not said to be "in the Branches." Nine are "below" (**hia**) and One "above" (**shang**); a remark as true today as it ever was.

The "Morea" (about fifty miles long), in Greece, was so named because it was supposed to resemble the leaf of a **morus** or mulberry. And similarly North America was considered by Mexican and Chinese mythologists to exhibit some resemblance to a mulberry,—the Helpful Mulberry (or **Fu-Sang**). The one comparison is just as fanciful or reasonable as the other. Nor can it be denied that North America presents some likeness to a Tree,—towering aloft like the Tree of the Prophet Daniel, which was seen from the ends of the earth. Here Columbia lights up her Tree and welcomes the Neighbors with a smile.

The Chinese note concerning the extra suns and moons, which frequently flit about and disappear, like so many sun-birds, connects them with the "Branches" of the Fu (or Fu-Sang) Tree of amazing proportions, which flourishes in the Region east of the Eastern Sea. The Fu-Sang land, 10,000 **le** (or 3,000 miles wide) is said to be 30,000 **le** (10,000 miles) to the east of China; and this indeed is the distance from Canton to California. A lesser distance (20,000 **le**, or 7,000 miles) lies between Northern China and the American Mulberry land due east. It is in America that we are directed to search for the surplus assemblage of suns. And do we not find both them and Fu-Sang? [Pg 5] (See note 10.) In what respect is the Chinese account inaccurate thus far? We are informed that "in the water is a large tree having nine suns," etc. The Trunk of this prodigious Tree, which is more or less immersed in the Eastern Sea, furnishes the surprising dimension of "300 **le**." And rising above a Valley of Hot Springs (readily found in Nicaragua) the Tree proceeds upward and rears aloft its exalted Branches in the "Place of the Ten Suns."

The vast mountain-system, with its tree-like "Trunk" and "Branches," on which the many suns and moons are seen to alight or gambol, is called the "Sun and Moon **shan**" (**shan** signifying "mountain or range") in both the Chinese text and the translation (see note 11.) It is identical with our continental stony Mulberry and constitutes the form of North America. Unfortunately our esteemed translator was utterly in the dark concerning the sense of the curious statements regarding the manifold suns and moons and even suggested that an explanation should be sought for in connection with the Philippine Islands. But the Tree, or range of the Sun and Moon, is plainly in North America. And here are the flocks of Suns roosting among the Branches.

## NOTICE OF OUR GRAND CANYON.

According to the translation, a "Great Canyon" is to be seen in the "Great Eastern Waste" "Beyond the Eastern Sea." And this Great Canyon is placed in connection with the "Sun and Moon shan",—which possesses the Mulberry's Branches and exhibit of Suns already glanced at (note 12.)

We read that a stream flows through this canyon, "producing a charming gulf." We are further informed that "the water accumulates and so forms a gulf. " A river flowing through the "Great Canyon," swells or widens out, displays a broadening expanse of water and becomes a Gulf, a "Charming Gulf."

Is not this the beautiful Gulf of California, which is a widening out or enlargement of a notable stream, the Colorado? Decidedly this mighty and famous river, whose "water accumulates and so forms a gulf," flows through a

Canyon. Moreover, this Canyon is truly a "Great Canyon." It is the greatest and grandest on the planet. It is also found in the "Great Waste to the east of the Eastern Sea," which washes the coast of China. It is the Grand Canyon of the Colorado.

The translation informs us (note 13) that this stream which flows into, or becomes a gulf has a "delightful spring. " The Canyon "has a beautiful mountain, from which there flows a delightful spring, producing a charming gulf. The water accumulates and so forms a gulf. " Such is the translation; but no Chinese term for "spring" appears in the text. The original states that it is a **kan shui** which runs through the Canyon, and this identical compound is translated "Sweet River" by our author on page 163 of his large and comprehensive work. **Kan** indeed signifies sweet, sweetness; delightsome, pleasant, happy, refreshing; and **Shui** stands for "water or river" (see Williams dict. pp. 310, 781.) It is therefore evident that a **kan shui** should be remarkable for the sweetness of its water and should start from a "delightful spring" of **sweet** water, in order to be pure and deserve its reputation. [Pg 6]

As a geographical fact, the Colorado flows out of the very fount which curiously enough, gives birth to the "Sweet Water." This stream becomes the Platte or Nebraska river, which joins the Missouri. And from the fount of the Sweet Water, exactly on the mountain divide, a head-stream of the Colorado bubbles out, enlarging into the affluent known as the "Green," the stream traverses the Grand Canyon and connects with the Gulf. (note 14.)

It should have a spring of **kan shui** or **sweet water**; and we find that it comes sparkling down the mountains from a **Sweet Water** spring.

The Sweet Water stream after traversing a Canyon, even a "Great Canyon" should connect with, or enlarge into, a gulf, described as "charming." Can the Gulf of California be regarded as charming?

One explorer expresses himself as charmed and delighted with the scenery

of the gulf. A sample passage in his report reads as follows: "The island and mountain peaks, whose outlines, as seen from the gulf, had been somewhat dimmed by a light haze, appeared surprisingly near and distinct in the limpid medium through which they were now viewed. The whole panorama became invested with new attractions, and it would be hard to say whether the dazzling radiance of the day or the sparkling clearness of the night was the more beautiful and brilliant. (note 15.)

Truly a charming and beautiful Gulf is here.

Although the translation does not draw attention to the fact, the term employed in the Chinese record to describe the course of the stream which passes through the Great Canyon, is **chu**. Now this word is employed to designate water which is "shooting over a ledge" (Williams' dict. p. 89), and its use is entirely appropriate in a description of the course of the water in the channel of the Colorado. The bed of the stream is exceedingly irregular and consists indeed of a succession of **ledges**—producing a series of rapids, falls, or cataracts. Were the water to disappear, the exposed bed of the Colorado, with its ascending series of steps, might be likened indeed with truth to a stairway for giants or gods.

The falls caused by **ledges (chu)** are exceedingly numerous. One navigator's log contains many such entries as the following: "Still more rapids and falls today. In one, the Emma Dean [a boat] is caught in a whirlpool, and set spinning about (n. 16).

One subdivision of the Grand Canyon is known as Cataract Canyon, and this section "in its 41 miles, has 75 rapids and cataracts, and 57 of these are crowded into 19 miles, with falls, in places, of 16 to 20 feet" (n. 17.)

All accounts concur in representing the stream as remarkable for the fury and number of its falls. To ascend the Colorado is a sheer impossibility and even to descend the stream is an enterprise rarely indeed attempted or achieved. Only rafts or life-boats, backed by pluck and luck, stand a chance of getting through—in pieces. The mariners all wear life-belts and are just as often in the water as they are out of it. Evidently a River of **Ledges** is here. Surely the term **Chu** (or water shooting over **Ledges**) applies with peculiar force to the career of this "wildest of rivers"—the Colorado.

[Pg 7]

## THE COLORADO— BOTTOMLESS?

Knowing quite well as we do, that our mighty river possesses a very substantial bottom composed of step-like ledges of rock, we learn with surprise that it is said to flow through a section described as **bottomless!** Is not such a statement or assertion absurd? But what did the ancient writer mean? What could he have meant?

The translation states that, according to a poem, the **Tsang-shan-wu**, "in the east there is a stream flowing in a **bottomless** ravine. It is supposed to be this Canyon"—the "Great Canyon of the Region beyond the Eastern Sea."

The Chinese term rendered "Canyon" is **Hoh**, which stands also for "a bed of a torrent, a deep gully or wady; a valley" (see Williams dict. p. 453.)

Of course, a **Ta** (or "Great") **Hoh** ought to be a Great Canyon, or a remarkable deep gorge or valley containing the bed of a torrent.

We have already been informed that a **Chu** (or river of ledges and falls) is in the **Ta Hoh**, or mighty gorge beyond the Eastern Sea. We also perceive that the title **Ta Hoh** applies properly to the mountain-hemmed course of our Colorado (which connects with Middle Park and runs to the Gulf.)

Somewhere in this immense and peerless **Ta Hoh**—somewhere among the majestic mountains—somewhere along the bed of the Colorado (either inside or outside of Middle Park,) the investigator should find a section which is **bottomless**. The ancient account locates it there. Nor are we to look for it in any Philippine Island. We are restricted to the bed or banks of the Colorado which we have identified as the **Chu** or plunging river that rushes downward to

the Gulf. Our leaping stream flows into and out of Grand Lake (within Middle Park.) Now this Lake (or enlargement of the bed of the Grand Colorado) "has a beach, and far out into the body of the water a sandy bottom" and "in the center, covering an area of nearly a **mile** square the Lake to all appearance is **bottomless.**"

We are further informed that "explorations of the edges of this great submarine cavern give the most positive evidences that it was once the crater of a great volcano" (note 18).

"The Lake to all appearance is bottomless. The deepest soundings that could ever be made have failed to reach bottom. Hence it is concluded that it has **no bottom.**"

Turn these two words, "no bottom" into Chinese and we get **wu ti**,—the very terms employed in the Chinese account.

No bottom, say the Ancients.

No bottom, say the Moderns.

The old account puts the unfathomable abyss in a **Kuh** (valley or ravine) and it is within a Valley—the Valley of Middle Park—that we actually find it. Moreover, this bottomless valley is "supposed" (or reported) to belong to the **Ta Hoh**—a title which would cover both Valley and Canyon. Indeed, Middle Park, with its enormous mountain-walls connects directly with the system of the Grand Canyon. Moreover, the one stream flows through both. And here it may be remarked that the **Chu** (or River of Ledges and Falls) is not termi [Pg 8] nated or swallowed up by the Bottomless abyss in **Kuh** (or Valley of Middle Park.) It flows on through the **Ta Hoh** and ultimately enlarges into a Gulf (the Gulf of California).

The rocky floor of the **Kuh** (or Valley of Middle Park) evidently constitutes a support or bottom for an impetuous and important River of Ledges or rapids and yet, at the same time, is reported to be Bottomless. This seems contradictory. But reaching the precise locality referred to in the old account, modern scientists simply echo the declaration of the Ancients,—that this Val-

ley or **Kuh**, traversed by a leaping, furious **Chu**, is unfathomable.

Bottomless! say the Ancients.

Bottomless! say the Moderns.

It thus appears that a statement seemingly calculated at first sight to drown the ancient claim in a flood of derision, turns out on examination to be overwhelmingly powerful evidence in support of the validity of the old record.

In no respect or degree is the ancient testimony contradicted or falsified by modern evidence. Take for instance the old assertion that the **shan** or mountain-range of the Great Canyon, is "beautiful." Nothing seems more natural than to conclude that such a laudatory term is grossly out of place and that the Mountain-range, with its Canyon and furious **Chu**, is a frightful, gloomy, dangerous, horrible, repulsive, bleak, and ugly mass of shattered and tottering heights. And, indeed, there is much truth in this view of the situation. Nevertheless, modern visitors unite in declaring that Beauty is a marked feature of the rocky heights that possess or direct the Colorado; and this is in agreement with the ancient account.

One traveler says: "The roar of its waters was heard unceasingly, . but its walls and cliffs, its peaks and crags, its amphitheatres and alcoves, tell a story of **beauty** and sublimity" (note 19).

Another visitor, who was treated most disrespectfully by our **Chu**, has eyes only for its "beauty": "The Canyon grows more and more picturesque and **beautiful** the farther we proceed. On many of the long stretches where the river can be seen for several miles, the picture is one of charming **beauty**. As the clouds rose we were treated to scenes rare and **beautiful** in the extreme" (n. 20.)

Again: "Cataract and Narrow Canyons are wonderful, Glen Canyon is **beautiful**, Marble Canyon is mighty; but it is left for the Grand Canyon, where the river has cut its way down through the sandstones, the marbles, and the granites of the Kaibab Mountains, to form those **beautiful** and awe-inspiring pictures that are seen from the bottom of the black granite gorge, where above us rise great wondrous mountains of bright red sandstone capped with cathedral domes and spires of white, with pinnacles and turrets, and towers, in such intricate forms and flaming colors that words fail to convey any idea of their **beauty** and sublimity."

The translation informs us that the mighty gorge is the Canyon of **Kiang, Shang**, or Almighty God.

And a modern visitor declares that "here Omnipotence stands revealed," and that here is "a glorious creation of God." (n. 21.) [Pg 9]

So impressed were the ancients with the beauty and grandeur of this region that they peopled it with the souls of illustrious sages, and declared that here was the Canyon of Almighty God. And those who enter it today, come reeling back from its portals,—declaring that no mortal can describe its glories, and that it is the Grand Canyon of Almighty God!

Words fail one in the attempt to describe this glorious creation of God. The impression it leaves upon the mind is overpowering. One feels as though he had been admitted into the presence of the Genii of the plutonic regions, had penetrated to the very heart of the inner world of elemental creations."

We need not wonder that the old account connects a revered ancestor with this glorious and celestial retreat in the Grand Canyon. He is called **Shao Hao**, and is furthur termed a **ju**, (or sucking child.)

**Shao** signifies "little" or "a little," and **Hao** is formed of the signs for "sun" and "heaven." It is therefore evident that the **ju** or infant at the Canyon is (or was) a little sun child, or child of the sun.

American rulers called themselves "Children of the Sun," and we should be careful not to confound our Arizona Prince with any Asiatic ruler. [The **Hao** or **Shao Hao** of supposed Chinese origin is represented by some different symbols: see Williams' dict. p. 172, columns 1 and 2.]

The little Child of the Sun at the **Ta-Hoh** or Great Canyon should not be—must not be—confounded with any early Chinese sun-worshiper. We are to look **far to the east of China** for both the Canyon and the little Child of the Sun referred to in the account before us.

We are informed that the country connected with the Great Canyon was called "**Shao Hao's** country" (or the land of the Sun-child) on account of the little Prince. He entered (**chi**) it, and this furnished the **reason** (or **chih**) for its title—Land of the Sun-child.

The infant (or **ju**) is distinctly called a ruler (or **ti**.) Moreover, although he was little (**shao**) or but a **ju** (suckling); he was a supreme king (or **chwen suh**). (Note 22.)

**Chwen** is formed by putting together the two words "only" and "head." And **suh** is a Chinese term composed of the two significant words "only" and "king" (see Williams' dict. pp. 117, 825, 1043.)

Evidently the baby ruler (or **ju ti**) was regarded by his people, in this region remarkable for its mountains, as the only or supreme head—the **chwen suh**, as Chinese historians might forcibly phrase it—of the people ruled.

[Because the infant was king and even the supreme king, it seems reasonable to suppose that his father was dead (and his mother alive) at the time when he was carried into the Great Canyon and duly suckled there.] We need not just here attempt to unravel his history. Enough to show that our Grand Canyon is positively and clearly referred to in Chinese literature. We may, however, note the fact that the royal infant (see translation) belonged to the **Kin Tien** or Golden Heaven family, and this title must be considered when the history of our Arizona Prince comes to be investigated. It should further be remarked that the respected translator has erred slightly in his supposition that the **Chwen Suh** (or Supreme Head) was "Shao Hao's descendant". [Pg 10] The Chinese terms in the original are: **shao hao** (not hao's) **ju** (baby) **ti** (ruler) **chwen suh** (head king.) It was the **little sun child ruler and supreme king** who was at the Canyon.

Particular attention should be paid to the fact, that, although regarded as a supreme ruler, the Prince is represented as being but a suckling (or **ju**) when in the neighborhood of the Great Canyon.

Now, the translation states that this baby or supreme lord "of whom no further description is given, **left there his lute** and lyre. It says that **his lute** and lyre are in this canyon."

## MUSIC IN THE GRAND CANYON?

It is absurd to imagine for a moment that a **sucking** infant could own, or could be really supposed to own, a **lute**. The Chinese text does not say that the musical instrument is "his." And yet, curiously enough, it does declare that the baby-prince left or abandoned (**k'i**) a Lute or Lyre in the Canyon.

Why should such a matter be mentioned? Supposing that a fiddle was left behind, or a drum, or a rattle, why should the trivial fact be gravely recorded?

If a Lute was left in the mighty chasm, its remains might be there still. But how could an infant be said to leave or abandon a Lute? Would he not try, so well as our memory serves, to first get it into his mouth? Would not his chubby hands, quite stout enough for destructive arts, tear the strings apart and feed the music to the nearest cat? Would it be a lute at all when ultimately relinquished? And if the babe derived pleasure from ill-treated and squalling strings, why should he leave the lute behind? As well say that the suckling abandoned there a fishing-rod! Would not a milk-bottle be a much readier fount of ecstacy than either a lute or a flute? Why, neither one nor the other **could be heard** within the Canyon.

A Chinese commentator, however, relieves us from the necessity of seeking for a literal lute between the resounding jaws of the mighty chasm (note 23.) He says it is erroneous (**ngo**) to suppose that the baby emperor (**ju ti**) grasped (**ping**,) or left behind (**chi**) or abandoned in the place of midnight darkness (**huen**) any lutes or lyres (**kin seh**.) In hyperbolical language (**wu wu**)—which is never true when taken literally—a clear limpid river (**shuh**) would be the lute (**kin**.)

But how could a clear stream serve as a lute?

The running water might produce limpid notes. Thus Moore, in his ode on "Harmony," uses the following words:

"Listen!—when the night-wind dies
Down the still current, **like a harp** it sighs!
A liquid **chord** in every wave that flows."

Here is a current of water likened to the string of a harp, and the playing of winds compared to music.

Mrs. Sigourney calls Niagara a "Trump," and we accept the assertion (although literally it is quite untrue.) [Pg 11]

But if the Chinese account placed a Trump in the Ontario chasm there would be considerable difficulty in finding it.

Fortunately, in the case immediately before us, it is a Chinese author who tells us that we are to seek for limpid streams rather than for literal lutes or lyres.

The mention of the latter would probably imply that the sounds of some stream or streams in the Great Canyon are of a remarkably soft and musical character.

Streams may produce delightful tones. Thus one observer (at Yellowstone) tells of the "mysterious music of the distant falls" "like the tremulous vibration of a mighty but remote harp-string." (note 24)

If falling water under certain peculiar acoustic circumstances can produce notes like those struck off from harp-strings, the tones can also be compared to those of lutes or lyres (for all are stringed instruments.)

The very volume which places lutes and lyres in the Great Canyon, also tells of a forest elsewhere, which is a "Forest of Lutes and Lyres" (note 25.)

Of course sounds merely resembling those of the stringed instruments, are here referred to. A forest is composed of trees rather than musical instruments, but it may produce musical tones like those of Lutes and Lyres.

And similarly the notes arising from the Grand Canyon may be of a lute-like character. This is the teaching of the Ancients. We have found the Bottomless stream and it is certain that visitors should return with accounts of melody arising from the Canyon. Future explorers should listen for musical notes. They will certainly not be disappointed.

One visitor says: "The waters waltz their way through the Canyon, making their own rippling, rushing, roaring music." We further read of innumerable cascades adding their wild music to the roar of the river."

What are these innumerable cascades but the strings of the Lute which was heard ages ago by enraptured ears and which has kept on resounding ever since. The concert in the Canyon drowns even the basic roar of the river. The music is there.

"We sit on some overhanging rocks, and enjoy the scene for a time, listening to the music of falling waters away up the canyons." (n. 26.)

It appears that the acoustic properties of the Grand Canyon are calculated to produce most notable effects: "Great hollow domes are seen in the eastern side of the rock. Our words are repeated with startling clearness, but in a soft mellow tone, that transforms them into magical music."

Elsewhere an immense grotto "was doubtless made for an academy of **music** by its storm born architect; so we name it **Music** Temple." (n. 27.)

Lutes and Lyres are there, say the Ancients.

A Temple of Music is there, say the Moderns.

It will be noticed that the Chinese annotater calls the Great Canyon—the **Ta Hoh**—a place of (**huen**) midnight darkness and declares that it is erroneous to suppose that the Lute played down there (where it could not possibly be heard) was an instrument held by a human hand (the hand of a suckling!). [Pg 12] Now, although the great gorge is wonderfully beautiful, it must be conceded that its basic part (within which human beings might dwell) is decidedly dark. Here "it is necessary to 'lie down upon one's back in order to see the sky,'—as I once heard General Crook express it. Into much of this deep gorge no ray of sunshine ever falls, and it well deserves the name of the 'Dark Canyon.'" (n. 28). Often in midday, stars are seen shining overhead; and it may well be called a place of midnight darkness (**huen.**)

In the following passage a modern visitor notices the "dark and frowning" walls of the chasm, but still enlarges on their beauty:—"One would think that after traveling through six hundred miles of those canyons, one would be satisfied with **beauty** and grandeur, but in this fact lies the charm. Of the six hundred miles no two miles are alike. The picture is ever changing from grandeur to beauty, from beauty to sublimity, from the **dark** and **frowning** greatness of its granite walls, to the dazzling colors of its upper cliffs. And I stood in the last few miles of the Grand Canyon spellbound in wonder and admiration, as firmly as I was fixed in the first few miles in surprise and astonishment." (note 29.)

Nature has done her best to adorn the walls of the mighty gorge. We are told of "**thousands of rivulets**" that "dropped farther and farther down, till the whole of the bright scarlet walls seemed hung with a tapestry of silver threads, the border fringed with white fleecy clouds which hung to the tops of the walls, and through which the points of the upper cliffs shone as scarlet tassels."

Nor was Dame Nature completely satisfied with her tapestry and fringe of tassels. Other embroidery was displayed. "As the sun broke through some side gorge, the canyon was spanned from side to side, as the clouds shifted their position, with rainbow after rainbow, vying to outdo in brilliancy of color the walls of the canyon themselves."

The ancient account declares, that in "the Region beyond the Eastern Sea," a Bottomless river traverses a Great Canyon. And this stream, remarkable for its ledges (**chu**) or rapids and falls, rushes onward and downward, and grows or enlarges into a Gulf. And the Canyon, the River, and the Gulf are all reported to be **Kan**—or **Beautiful**.

And visitors today return from all three, declaring that they are Beautiful! Beautiful!! Beautiful!!!

And some are entranced by strains of music arising from the mouth of the Canyon and declare that it holds an "orchestra." In one place the thousands of streamlets, glistening and gleaming like silvery cords, stretch downward from the edge of the painted chasm; and the resounding, melodious precipice is called "the Cliff of the Harp." (note 30. ) What is this but an echo of the ancient declaration that the royal Lute in the Canyon was merely a musical stream. Similar ideas have occurred to poets. Coleridge in his "Ancient Mariner," tells of

"A noise like of a hidden brook
　In the leafy month of June,
Which to the sleeping woods all night
　Singeth a quiet tune."
[Pg 13]

And Moore has heard the notes of harp-strings sounding forth from melodious streams. What wonder, then, that ancient poets (and the translation states that the particular work which makes mention of the "Bottomless **Kuh**" or valley, is a "poem") should have likened a collection of falling streams or cascades to the chords of a tuneful Lute and then, to distinguish it from others less excellent, have applied to the stringed instrument the name of their Prince. Americans today gravely talk of visiting or seeing "St. Luke's Head" (in California!) And we possess a mere natural formation which is supposed to resemble a nose and is religiously called "St. Anthony's Nose." In truth this "nose" is no more a literal nose than the "Lute" in the Canyon is a literal stringed instrument made by men. Then we have "Cleopatra's Bath" and "Pompey's Pillar." (Next tell us in the interest of chaos and confusion that Pompey left here "his" Pillar.)

In the grand caves at Pikes Peak there is an "organ," which is really no organ at all. It is a natural formation or production from which charming melodies are fetched by skilled musicians. Now if we ourselves can gravely call a musical,

highly-strung rock an "Organ," may not the Ancients be excused for calling a combination of musical streams a Lute? Contemplating the "Cliff of the Harp," we can readily understand how old-time visitors found down there the tuneful string of a "Lute" and how an imperial Child of the Sun was unable to lug along "his" notable musical toy. There it remains and melodious notes still come floating up.

Lutes and Lyres are there, say the Ancients.

"An Academy of Music!" say the Moderns.

The Chinese annotater remarks that the **lieh tsze** (a class of sages or teachers—the literati) are unacquainted (**pu chi**) with the **sheu-hai** or Gulf situated toward the east (**chi tung**.)

The Chinese scholars of the writer's time knew little or nothing of our Gulf of California (or **Sheu-hai**). However, it was known to some; and we are now informed that it is ki (a **few**; nearly about, approximately) **yih** (to **guess**, to bet; 100,000; an indeterminate number) **wan** (10,000) **le**.

A single **wan le** should measure about 3,000 miles, and a **few** (to "guess") separate China from the **Ta-Hoh** which connects with the Bottomless **kuh** or valley ("**Ta-Hoh shih wei wu ti chi kuh**.)

Evidently the Great Canyon lies more than **one wan le** (3,000 miles) to the east of China. We find indeed that the number may well be referred to as "a few" (**ki**.)

Nor can the Gulf be **more** than about 30,000 **le** to the east, seeing that this Gulf of California is in "the region beyond the Eastern Sea" along with the **Fu-Tree** which has a trunk of 300 **le**. The Gulf to the east is connected with the mountain system whose Branches exhibit the gorgeous spectacle of Ten Suns. In short, the Gulf and Canyon are along with **Fu-Sang**; and **Fu-Sang** is only 30,000 **le** to the east of China, and merely 10,000 wide. Accordingly, the Gulf is but "a few" **wan le** to the east of the Flowery Kingdom.

To look for the Canyon and Tree within the Philippine Islands, contigu-

ous to China, is simply impossible. The islands have been pretty well thrashed [Pg 14] over lately, and no one has met with the Tree! It has a "Trunk of 300 le," and collectors of curios or strange plants should keep wide awake and see that they don't pass it in the dark. And yet with its Ten Moons, how miss it? How fail to notice our glittering, gleaming, glorious candelabrum? It couldn't have fallen or drifted over to the Panama ditch? It can't possibly be now stuck in any South American Flower-pot? Catching the Tree seems to be as slippery as catching Tartars, and perhaps when the first is found, the others won't be very far off.

The Chinese commentator, of course, never saw either the Gulf or Canyon but he quotes from earlier writers who were well acquainted with our "region beyond the Eastern Sea;" and one of these named **Chwangtsze**, is quoted to the effect that in the **Ta Hoh** or Great Canyon **high winds** (**yuen fung**) occur (**yu**) or come unexpectedly upon one.

Do storms arise suddenly in the neighborhood of the mighty chasm?

One modern explorer says: "I go up to explore the alcove. While away a whirlwind comes scattering the camp fire among the dead willows and cedar spray and soon there is a conflagration, the men rushing for the boats, leaving all they cannot readily seize at the moment, and even then they have their clothing burned and hair singed." (note 31.)

Storms occur in all parts of the world. Is there anything peculiar about the tempests which are said to suddenly arise in the Great Canyon?

One visitor says: "Storms were not infrequent and these occurring where the canyon walls were a mile high and close together produced an effect that was almost supernatural in its awfulness. The deep thunder echoed sharply between the cliffs, producing a roaring sound that was almost deafening." (note 32.)

It should be remembered that the vast caverns here multiply the bellowings of thunder and also help to confine and intensify the raging and imprisoned whirlwinds.

One eye or ear witness tells of a storm both seen and heard within the Canyon and adds: "I have seen the lightning play and heard the thunder roll among the summit peaks of the Rocky Mountains, as I have stood on some rocky point far above the clouds, but **nowhere** has the awful grandeur equalled that night in the lonesome depths of what was to us death's canyon. Again all was shut in by darkness thicker than that of Egypt. The stillness was only broken by the roar of the river as it rushed along beneath me. Suddenly as if the mighty cliffs were rolling down against each other, there was peal after peal of thunder striking against the marble cliffs below, and mingling with their echoes, bounding from cliff to cliff. Thunder with echo, echo with thunder, crossed and recrossed from wall to wall of the canyon," etc. (note 33.)

Surely sudden and dreadful storms rage here. The loudest in North America, says an expert.

Observe that the visitor just quoted notices the "roar of the river" in connection with the fury of the tempest.

Now, the ancient visitor does the same. After directing attention to the sudden high winds, he says that a decidedly curious sight or spectacle (**king** [Pg 15] **shun**) is the **keang** (a large main stream which receives tributaries) spreading abroad (**fu**) the **noise** of flowing water (**tsung**) in the **Ta-Hoh** or Great Canyon.

The noise of the great river or **Keang** is thus noticed by the ancient visitor, who also declares that the **Ta-Hoh** or Great Canyon constitutes a decidedly fine or curious sight.

And such in truth it actually is. "Imagine a chasm that at times is less than a quarter of a mile wide and more than a mile deep, the bed of which is a tossing, **roaring**, madly impetuous flood. What an imposing spectacle; what a sublime vision of mightiness!" (n. 34).

A great sight! say the Ancients.

A Wonder of the World! say the Moderns.

The roar of the river has never ceased since the ancient scribe, or his informant, passed that way. A modern visitor says: "The threatening **roar** of the water is loud and constant."

Again, "The **roar** of its waters was heard unceasingly from the hour we entered it until the time we landed here. No quiet in all that time." (n. 35).

One navigator tells of a "bore" in connection with the resounding stream. "In the stillness of the night, the roaring of the huge mass could be heard reverberating among the windings of the river. This singular phenomenon of the 'bore,' as it is called, is met with but at few places in the world. In the course of four or five hours the river falls about thirty feet" (n. 36.)

Another explorer pauses at one spot in his amphibious career to note that "high water mark" can be seen "fifty, sixty, or a hundred feet above its present stage;" and "when a storm bursts over the canyon, a side gulch is dangerous, for a sudden flood may come and the inpouring waters will raise the river, so as to hide the rocks before your eyes" (n. 37).

Another navigator, who never was without a life-belt,—which he found of vital use when righting his too often overturned ark,—tells with amazement of "the waves, torrents, and cataracts of this wildest of rivers."

A ceaseless basic roar is there,—deadened at times by floods of music, yet nevertheless eternally there.

The sea connected with the Great Canyon is elsewhere called a **Puh hai** (the latter term signifying "sea.")

A **Puh hai** is said to be a "Gulf," and we find a Gulf—the Gulf of California—at the mouth of the Colorado.

It should, however, be observed that the term **Puh** by itself stands for "an arm of the sea." A **Puh hai** is a Gulf which forms "an arm of the sea." The Gulf or sea should be shaped like an **arm**—an arm of the ocean (see Williams' dict. p. 718.)

Now, a glance at the map shows that in a very peculiar sense the Gulf of California is a **hai** or "sea" which meets the requirements of being shaped like an

**arm**. It is a sea and a gulf and at the same time "an arm" of the ocean. Truly it is a **Puh hai**.

A great many "gulfs" are quite unlike "arms," being too broad to admit [Pg 16] of such a comparison. But our Gulf of California is comparatively narrow and is truly an "arm" of the sea. And notice how the water of the river—our Colorado—"accumulates and so forms a gulf." Such are the words of the existing translation and they apply completely to the American situation. Here we find the water of the Colorado accumulating or widening out until it becomes a great body of water—a Gulf. Indeed this development or process of expansion is so gradual that it is impossible for navigators to tell where the river ends or the gulf begins.

In the Chinese comment immediately before us, however, the **hai** or sea to the Canyon's river mouth is called a **Sheu**.

Now this term signifies "to rinse the mouth, to scour; to wash out a thing; to purify." (Williams, p. 757.)

The word **Sheu** is written by combining the characters for "water" and "to suck in."

It is evident that our Gulf of California is "an arm of the sea" and no less a **Sheu**. A "mouth" it undoubtedly has, and this mouth is being ceaselessly "washed," "scoured," and "purified." Even a dentist would be satisfied! The immense stream rushes out, and tides from the Pacific rush in. Moreover the Colorado "sucks in" the tidal wave known as the Bore. Surely we have here the Eastern Gulf sea which is both a **Puh** and a **Sheu**.

The water of the noisy, restless, purifying stream within the **Ta-Hoh** was it is said,—

1. **Yu** (which means "used or employed.")

2. **Wuh** (to water or irrigate; to soften with water; to enrich.)

3. **Tsiao** (scorched, burned, singed, dried up.)

4. **Chi** (referring to or denoting.)

5. **Tsze** (here or this.)

Evidently the water of the Colorado was used to **irrigate** some ground or vegetation which was dried up or scorched.

Such a remark implies a high temperature (during the period of growth) between the walls of the chasm, and also leads us to look for some soil—some scorched or dried up soil (sadly in need of irrigation)—between the jaws of the Canyon. Is there parched or desert soil on the banks of the Colorado?

Here is the answer: "The region through which the chafing waters of the Colorado run is forbidding in the extreme, a vast **Sahara** of waste and inutility; a desert too dreary for either vegetable or animal life; a land that is **haunted with wind-storm**, on which ride the furies of desolation. The earth is **parched to sterility**. It is like the moon, a **parched** district, save for the single stream which, instead of supplying sustenance, is eating its vitals." (note 38.)

Another traveler visited Fort Yuma, on the Colorado, and says: "The ride to the fort was through a flat and desolate looking country. It was a dreary eight hours ride." Other remarks are made concerning "the barrenness of the surrounding region and" "the **intense heat** of its summer climate." (note 39.) [Pg 17]

In some spots, however, water produces magical effects. In the Mojave valley, for instance, "the annual overflow of the river enables the Mojaves, to raise with little labor, an abundant supply of provisions for the year. During one season, a few years since, the Colorado did not overflow its banks; there were consequently no crops and great numbers of the Mojaves perished from starvation." (note 40.)

Curiously enough, although rain fell furiously within the Canyon, it was observed by a traveler that "such rainstorms were invariably confined to the immediate vicinity of the Canyon, the territory lying two or three miles east or west continuing parched with hardly a cloud above it." And the explorer wonders how some ancient inhabitants, whose buildings are now in ruins, "managed to exist, situated as they were in a desolate country, where there was great scarcity of both vegetable and animal life."

The ancient Chinese account connects a baby king, a supreme ruler, with the Great Canyon and now states that water was used within the gorge to irrigate the soil, which is represented as being dried up or scorched. Is the Canyon remarkable for its heat? Surely it ought to be cool down there?

One visitor says: "That Canyon was the sultriest place I have ever struck, and my experience includes some of the hottest sections this side of the equator."

The oppressive heat in the chasm was felt at a "point fifty times as deep as the great chasm at Niagara." (note 41.)

"But despite the terrible heat, despite the discomfort of the situation, I was compelled to wonder and admire, For,"—

The **Ta-Hoh** should constitute a magnificent sight, but it is also said to contain some **scorched** or dried up soil. Is such to be seen?

An explorer reached the Colorado at a point where it is 266 yards wide, and adds that the "soil" "bore nothing but dry weeds and bushes and the whole scene presented the most perfect picture of desolation I have ever beheld, as if some **sirocco** had passed over the land, **withering** and **scorching everything**." (note 42.)

Withered and scorched! say the Ancients.

Withered and scorched! say the Moderns.

In one favored spot, "to the limit of vision, the tortuous course of the river (the Colorado) could be traced through a belt of alluvial land varying from one to six miles in width, and garnished with inviting meadows, with broad groves of willow and mezquite and promising fields of grain." The visitor remarks that the valley appears most attractive in the spring—"at this season of the year before the **burning heat** has **withered** the freshness and beauty of the early vegetation." (note 43.)

We are informed that the valley south of the Bend of the Colorado near the "Needles," there is in the spring a "most brilliant array" of flowers; but, "after the ephemeral influence of the few spring showers has passed, the annual

plants are soon **burned** up by the sun's heat and perfect sterility prevails throughout the remainder of the season. " (note 44.)

It is sufficiently apparent that the soil when properly watered can produce [Pg 18] abundant vegetation and sufficient nourishment for, of course, limited numbers of human beings. Deprived of water, the soil is unable to sustain desirable plants, and presents a sterile aspect. Surveying its present condition or appearance of barrenness, a modern visitor wonders how the ancient inhabitants contrived to exist, or find food, within the withered, unfruitful chasm. But one of the ancients, Mr. Chwang Tsze, writing about this very **Ta-Hoh** or Great Chasm, says that they used water to irrigate the otherwise scorched or dried up soil. Then, if such a somewhat belated answer is true, the question arises, where are the proofs?

A chief of the Ethnological Bureau very properly furnishes the answer. Standing in the abyss of the **Ta-Hoh**, on the bank of the roaring river, he beholds some ancient buildings and perceives how their vanished occupants formerly contrived to subsist. He says: "We can see where the ancient people who lived here—a race more highly civilized than the present—had made a **garden**, and **used** a great spring" [or feeder of the Colorado], "that comes out of the rocks for **irrigation**," etc. (n. 45.)

We irrigated the soil, say the Ancients.

They irrigated the soil, say the Moderns.

Next comes the statement of some trusted early sage or scholar who was certainly acquainted with our **Ta-Hoh** (containing the ruin and irrigated soil just noticed.) It is an observer or scribe named **Tu-tsan**, who says:—

10. **Seay** (to paint, to draw, to sketch. )

11. **yih** (to spread abroad, to diffuse.)

12. **tung** (a gorge, ravine, canyon, a cave, a grotto.)

13. **hueh** ("a hole in the earth or side of a hill,—they are used for dwellings;" a den, a grotto, a cavern.)

Something called **seay** is here said to

be spread abroad, or diffused over rocky walls or caves. Williams (p. 796) says that **seay** (or **sie** as it is also spelled) stands for a sketch or design, and adds that it means to draw, to compose, to write. Morrison, in his dictionary, says that **seay** signifies "to paint," etc.

Of course there is no use looking for anything so absurd as pictured or painted rocky walls or caves; and we accordingly feel disappointed when the ancient text seems to notice such. The pictures or paint should be "spread abroad" freely or lavishly in the vicinity of caverns, and we know positively that no "paint" or pigment of human composition can be seen on the canyon walls. No artificial pictures are there, and we are compelled to admit that the ancient account here stands falsified.

We have, however, found the caves. Music Temple, for instance measures two hundred feet from floor to roof, and is "a vast chamber carved out of the rock." There are caverns in all directions. And the noisy, roaring river is certainly there as well. One explorer says: "Imagine a chasm that at times is less than a quarter of a mile wide and more than a mile deep, the bed of which is a tossing, roaring, madly impetuous flood, winding its way in a sinuous course along **walls** that are **painted** with all the pigments known to nature. What an imposing spectacle!" (n. 46.) [Pg 19]

Of course we must object that the "walls" are really not walls and that the "paint" so lavishly spread upon them is not paint at all. The ancient assertion is delusive, but equally so is the modern. Just compare them.

The Virgin River enters the Colorado, and at the place of junction are the "resplendently **painted** temples and towers of the Virgin. Here the slopes, the serpentine ledges, and the bosses of projecting rock, interlarded with scanty soil, display all the colors of the rainbow, and in the distance may be likened to the **painter's pallete**. The bolder tints are of maroon, purple, chocolate, magenta, and lavendar, with broad bands of white laid in horizontal belts. (n. 47.)

Is this so-called "paint" **lavishly** "spread abroad"?

Certainly; one section of the mighty and wondrous gorge is known as "the **painted** canyon."

Of course the chasm is not really "painted" by artists or human agents, and we need not look for painted cliffs anywhere. Nevertheless modern observers echo the language of the ancients, and we are told today of "the **painting** of the rocks" and of "deep, **painted** alcoves" and "**painted** grottos" (n. 48.)

The term **yih** (see Williams' dict. pp. 781, 1092) is composed of the characters for "fluid" and "vessel," and signifies "A vessel full to the brim; ready to overflow, to run over; abundant; to spread abroad, to diffuse." As **seay**, the word which precedes **yih** in our Chinese note, signifies "to paint," we perceive how the additional term **yih** teaches that the **paint** made use of has been applied to extensive surfaces, so that it presents the appearance of having "overflowed" or "run over" the rocky walls and caverns dealt with.

Of course neither writing nor literal pictures could overflow or drench—and adhere to—walls or cliffs. But **seay yih** might cover the motion of applying **paint** in a most lavish, copious, overflowing manner. Here are cliffs so "rich with parti-coloring as to justify the most extravagant language in describing them."

It looks as though the gnomes on the job, in the Canyon, just emptied their paint-pots down dizzy cliffs and then went back for more. And such extravagance is in harmony with the symbols which stand for painting and vessels and spreading abroad or overflowing! Mineral paints were freely used and sometimes apparently with considerable care and skill. Thus we read of a red sandstone cliff "unbroken by cracks or crevices or ledges" exhibiting "extensive flat surfaces beautifully **stained** by iron, till one could imagine all manner of tapestry effects."

Here are painted imitations of tapestry.

It should further be remembered that

there are actual picture writings spread abroad on extensive painted or stained surfaces. The author just quoted beheld ancient dwellings which "exhibited considerable skill on the part of the builders, the corners being plumb and square." And just here "there were also numerous picture writings." (note 49.)

An amazed visitor exclaims: "Grand, glorious, sublime, are the Pictorial cliffs of vermillion hue!" [Pg 20]

"Pictorial" answers to **seay** (the 10th character in our list.)

Pictured and painted! say the Ancients.

Pictured and painted! say the Moderns.

We have seen that our Gulf (of California) has been called a **Puh-hai**, or "arm of the sea."

Professor Hoith, the celebrated student of Chinese, in his work on "Chinese History" (p. 49, footnote) says that a **puh hai** is "an estuary."

Webster says that an "estuary" is "an arm of the sea; a firth; a narrow passage, or the mouth of a river or lake, where the tide meets the current, or flows and ebbs."

Plainly our Gulf of California is a **Puh hai** or Estuary.

It may further be remarked that **Puh** is written in Chinese by putting together two characters, one standing for "water," and the other signifying "Suddenly; hastily; flurried, disconcerted, as when caught doing wrong; to change color, confused" (Williams' dict. p. 718. )

It is superfluous to say that our Gulf or Estuary is a very "confused" or "flurried" body of water. It is truly a **Puh-hai**.

Moreover, it "changes color." As though "caught doing wrong," it changes color and blushes at times a rosy red. This is the hue of multidunious veins: "A thousand streams rolling down the cliffs on every side, carry with them red sand; and these all unite in the canyon below, in one great stream of red mud" (n. 50.) But sometimes the color below Yuma is yellow or black (n. 51.)

The name "Colorado" is a Spanish

term conveying the idea of redness, and undoubtedly this hue predominates throughout the course of the boisterous stream; but other colors due to the dye or wash of variously painted cliffs, are also met with. Moreover a section may exhibit one color to-day and something different to-morrow. And so it is with the gulf, which receives the Colorado, and on which floating patches of color are frequently seen. Truly our Gulf or Estuary is remarkable for both its coloring, blue, red, etc., and its changes of color. In all respects it is plainly a **Puh-hai**.

Our Gulf or Estuary is also called a **yuen**. Farther on (see Chinese version) we read that the Canyon river produces or grows into (**shang**) a beautiful (**kan**) **yuen**.

This term **yuen** stands for a "gulf, an abyss; an eddy, a whirlpool or place where the back water seems to stop."

A whirling, violent, or impetuous body of water is evidently referred to. Fernando Alarchon, in 1540, found the Colorado "a very mighty river, which ran with so great a fury of stream that we could hardly sail against it.

One voyager tells how his ark, the "Emma" was "caught in a **whirlpool**, and set spinning about." Here is a **yuen**.

Again, "The men in the boats above see our trouble but they are caught in whirlpools, and are spinning about in eddies."

What have we here but **Yuen**—multiplied whirlpools? [Pg 21]

Through "Whirlpool Canyon" and all the way to the Gulf, the waters dance around and about. We read of "dancing eddies or whirlpools." There are more than 600 rapids and falls in the Colorado (n. 52.)

The waters **waltz** their way and even furnish their own "rippling, rushing, roaring music." And we are in addition told of "innumerable cascades adding their wild music" (n. 53).

Surely the entire inlet traversed by the bore or reached by ocean tides is in precisely the condition of commotion which may well be designated by the term yuen.

We are informed that the **kan** (or

beautiful) **yuen** approaches (**tsih**) with vapor (**hi hwo**) and bathes (**yuh**) the sun's place (**ji chi su**).

It is evident that the mighty stream which traverses the Great Canyon in the region beyond the Eastern Sea, should flow from a Bottomless valley to a Gulf, and reach to the Sun's Place. And we find that the current of the Colorado extends to the Tropical line of Cancer, which crosses and marks the mouth of the Gulf of California.

Vapor or fog is noticed in connection with the beautiful (even if restless or reeling) Yuen.

Are fogs a noticeable feature along the coast of California? If so, they might hide the entrance or mouth of the Gulf.

One visitor says: "Westward toward the setting sun and the sea," was a "filmy fog creeping landward, swallowing one by one the distant hills."

Again, we read of "hilltops that thrust their heads through the slowly vanishing vapor."

Here "you may bask in the sunshine of gardens of almost tropic luxuriance or shudder in **fogs that shroud the coast**" (n. 54.)

We need not wonder that such vapors should appear within the confines of the charming Gulf of California and at times veil its shores. A recent visitor says: "The island and mountain peaks, whose outlines are seen from the Gulf, had been somewhat **dimmed** by a light **haze**, appeared surprisingly near and distinct in the limpid medium through which they were now viewed. The whole panorama became invested with new attractions, and it would be hard to say whether the dazzling radiance of the day or the sparkling clearness of the night was the more **beautiful** and brilliant" (n. 55).

Hazy and Beautiful, say the Ancients.
Hazy and Beautiful, say the Moderns.

The haze is not dense enough to blind our eyes to the manifest fact that those people of old who were acquainted with the position of our Gulf of California, must also have been acquainted with Mexico and its inhabitants.

Tropical America was considered by its people to be particularly under the

influence of the Sun. Uxmal was in "the Land of the Sun" (n. 56), and the Mexicans called themselves "Children of the Sun."

[Pg 22]

## CAVE DWELLINGS IN THE GRAND CANYON.

It will be noticed that the 13th term in our list is **hueh**, which stands for cave habitation. Are such to be seen in our Canyon?

Numerous **tung** (see 12th term,) in the shape of caves or holes are undoubtedly there, but in addition the old account notices **hueh**. Have such been found?

One explorer says: "Even more remarkable than the stupendous walls which confine the Colorado river, are the ruined cave habitations which are to be seen along the lofty and inaccessible ledges, in which a vanished race long years ago evidently sought refuge from their enemies. They were reached by very narrow, precipitous, and devious paths, and being extremely difficult to attain by the occupants themselves, presented an impregnable front to invaders" (n. 57.)

Explorers decending into the **ta-hoh** come forth to-day with accounts of gardens and irrigating streams, pictured cliffs, and cave dwellings,—in complete agreement with the ancient record.

Following the term **hueh** we find a 14th, called **han**, which stands for dry, heated air; too dry; parched as by drought; crisp.

Is there **han**, or dry heated air down in the Canyon?

One visitor entered the Grand Canyon "in the morning while darkness yet covered the scene, but even then it was oppressively hot, and as the sun got higher I felt as though I had been thrust into a dutch **oven** and the mouth stopped up. But, despite the terrible heat . I was compelled to wonder and admire . the gorgeous cliffs and rock walls showing all those varied colorings," etc. (n. 58).

It was the "terrible heat" which compelled the Ancients to resort to irrigation in order to raise some food for themselves and little ones. Destitute of water, the soil is scorched and barren.

It is said that "there are about 700 square miles of arable land between the mouth of the Gila and the 35th parallel of N. latitude," along the Colorado. And "in the valley" of this stream, where it is joined by the Gila, "are traces of ancient irrigating canals, which show that it has once been cultivated." And along the connected Gila are irrigating works of remarkable construction and undoubted antiquity—antedating the arrival of the Spaniards by centuries.

Where the soil is actually irrigated or cultivated the response of nature is most gratifying and encouraging. We learn with regard to the Colorado valley, that "portions are cultivated by the numerous tribes of Indians who live along its banks, affording them an abundance of wheat, maize, beans, melons, squashes," etc. (n. 59).

Such ground would be well worthy of attention; but the attitude of "the numerous tribes of Indians" along the Colorado might interfere with the plans of newcomers and even compel the latter to live in caves or on ledges easily defended. And it is certain that soil insufficiently watered presents a distressingly sterile aspect in the neighborhood of the Colorado.

One traveler, already quoted, says with regard to a wide section, that "the [Pg 23] whole scene presented the most perfect picture of desolation I have ever beheld, as if some Sirocco had passed over the land, **withering** and **scorching** everything to crispness" (n. 60.)

Notice this word "crispness" used by our author. Turned into Chinese it becomes **han** (crisp)—the very term applied in the ancient record to the condition of the soil unwatered within the Canyon. It is curious how the old and new visitors agree in their descriptions of the interior of the mighty gorge, where vegetation is withered or dead.

Scorched and Crisp! say the Ancients.

Scorched and Crisp! say the Moderns.

The Canyon should be hot, and one of our own visitors says: "The sun shone directly up the Canyon, and the glare **reflected from the walls** made the heat intolerable (n. 61.)

The word **han** has, unfortunately enough, a perfect right to appear in the old record. Following it we find additional terms:

15. A compound character consisting of the signs for "Sun" (**Jih**) and "People" (**Min**.)

16. **lung** ("used for **nagas** or snake gods;" "a dragon," "imperial." "It is often used for a man.")

17. **chuh** ("the illumination of torches; a candle; a light; to give or shed light upon, to illumine")

The statement seems to teach that the Sun People—the men—were using torches to illumine the depth of the hot Canyon.

We have already been informed that a **ju** or suckling, who was yet a supreme King (like perhaps the last Chinese Emperor of the Manchu dynasty, in 1912 A. D.) and a Child of the Sun, was down in the abyss, so we are prepared to hear that his subjects—some Sun people—were down there too.

Of course, for the greater part of the twenty-four hours, the darkness, particularly in the cave dwellings should be most intense. One visitor, quoted already, tells of "darkness thicker than that of Egypt." Such gloom should be particularly and painfully felt by "Sun People," and we are not surprised to find that they made use of torches or artificial lights. Singularly enough, the chasm, as though remorsefully conscious of the blackness of its character, produces no end of dried-up vegetable stems or stalks fit to be ignited and used as firebrands. These it places convenient to your hand, as though to invite inspection.

Indians today are in the habit of using such torches. We are informed that "the custom still prevails among them of carrying a firebrand," which was noticed by Spanish explorers in the 16th Century, "and induced those discoverers to give to the river the name of Rio del Tizon" (n. 62).

It will be noticed that the ancient Chinese account connects lights, or "an illumination of Torches" (**chuh**), with the very stream which the Spaniards of a later age, and of their own accord christened the Rio del Tizon.

A Torch-lighted stream, say the Chinese.

A Torch-lighted stream, say the Spaniards. [Pg 24]

The author or explorer last quoted says with reference to Indians dwelling on the banks of the Colorado, that "the custom still prevails among them of carrying a firebrand in the hand in cold weather," which was noticed by the Spaniards.

Of course the flaming brands may well be used in winter to warm those who hold them, but the Ancients who inhabited the cave or cliff houses (which they built and which are now more or less in ruin, according to exposure or original inherent strength) might have used the **chuh** or torches as **lights**. These torches are mentioned in connection with excessive **heat**, and it would be absurd to suppose that the Sun People of old desired a still higher temperature. But mention is made of cave dwellings, and such are actually there; and we can readily understand why the ancient dwellers in the cave houses should have frequently used the ready-to-hand torches when climbing to their dark and break-neck abodes.

Even today the **chuh** or torches are used as **lights**. The withered stalks or stems, so abundant in the Canyon, are a melancholy illustration of the scorching power of the sun within the chasm. We have not forgotten the fact that the Chinese term **han** is used in the ancient text and that it stands for the "crispness" of scorched or dried up plants. An actual visit to the **Ta-Hoh** or Great Canyon referred to, shows that it is this **han**— or withered, scorched and crisp—vegetation which provides no end of torches (**chuh**) for dwellers in the vicinity. One stumbling visitor uses the following language: "We struck for it . through the thick night, the guide occasionally lighting a **torch of grass**" (n. 63). Unable to directly or steadily illumine the angles or recesses of the Canyon, the bright and clear-headed sun does the next best thing and raises a bounteous harvest of firebrands. Nature here concentrates her attention on the task of serving the necks (rather than the bellies) of her children, and presents them with a crop of seasoned and brilliant torches. Certain it is that most efficient firebrands are raised here in profusion and constitute such a unique feature of the stream that in order to distinguish it from others in the region, the Spaniards called our river the Rio del Tizon. Torches have lighted the Canyon in the past and they now throw light on the ancient record.

Mentioned in connection with withered vegetation and intense heat, the natural inference is that the torches were used to **light** the steps of dwellers in the Canyon. Of course they might in winter have been used, like other vegetable produce, as fuel, but the old record now before us does actually connect the **chuh** or torches with a high scorching temperature; and our impression or deduction is that they were used as lights amid the blackness of the chasm.

And the Torches (**chuh**) are used as lights still. One explorer says: "We fear that we shall have to stay here clinging to the rocks until daylight. Our little Indian gathers a few dry stems, ties them in a bundle, lights one end, and holds it up. The **others do the same**, and with these **Torches** we **find a way** out of trouble."

Observe that these torches (or **chuh** as the Chinese would call them) were not ignited to **warm** the explorers. They were held aloft to find or light the way among perilous cliffs. Without their aid it would have been madness [Pg 25] for the explorers to move. Practically they were as men born blind, but the Indian guide, with knowledge derived from the depths of antiquity, obtains the necessary torches and light at his elbow. With one withered and hot stem he ties together a number, lights them and then finds the way out of trouble for both himself and his bewildered party. What have we here but a duplication of the "illumination of torches" referred to in the ancient record?

17. **chuh** (the illumination of torches;

a candle; a torch.)

18. **yuen** ("to lead or take by the hand, to cling to; to pull up higher, to drag out; to put forward; to relieve, to rescue")

19. **yiu** (have, has; to get.)

20. **Ta** (Great.)

21. **Hoh** (Canyon.)

22. **hao** (a mark, classed, a signal.)

23. **wei** (said or declared; has; in the place of.)

24. **wu** (no; without; destitute of.)

25. **te** (bottom.)

It appears that within the bottomless **Ta-hoh** or Great Canyon (see words 19 to 25) there is an illumination of torches (**chuh**) and a pulling up higher, or a dragging about and clinging to (**yuen**).

Climbing is here referred to. The Sun people seem to have found locomotion difficult and hazardous within the chasm.

The modern explorer who reached the irrigated garden plots and houses of the ancient occupants, was himself compelled to resort to much climbing. In one place he says: "I find I can get up no farther, and cannot step back, for I dare not let go with my hands, and cannot reach foot-hold below without. I call to Bradley for help. The moment is critical. Standing on my toes my muscles begin to tremble. I hug close to the rock, let go with my hand, seize the dangling legs, and with his assistance, I am enabled to gain the top" (n. 64.)

It will be seen by the intelligent reader that the forgoing performance is covered by the term **yuen** (No. 18) used in the ancient record. There was a **rescue** by Bradley, and the desperate adventurer, a chief of the Ethnological Bureau, was "pulled up higher," even to "the top" of the cliff. All this constitutes **yuen**; and without intending it, our modern climber—calling to Bradley for help—is a most eloquent and lucid commentator on the ancient statement in the Chinese text.

But this climbing should be accomplished in connection with **chuh** (No. 17—the illumination of torches). Is it true that there is climbing by torchlight (not **moonlight**, gentle reader) within the chasm?

Light is thrown on the ancient text by a statement already in part quoted: "We fear that we shall have to stay here **clinging** to the rocks until daylight. Our little Indian gathers a few dry stems, ties them in a bundle, lights one end, and holds it up. The others do the same, and with these torches we find a way out of trouble. **Helping** each other, holding **torches** for each other, one **clinging** to another's **hand** until we get footing, then supporting the other on [Pg 26] his shoulders, so we make our passage into the depths of the canyon. And now Captain Bishop has kindled a huge fire of driftwood, on the bank of the river. This and the fires in the gulch opposite, and our own **flaming torches**, light up little patches, that make more manifest the awful darkness below. Still, on we go, for an hour or two, and at last we see Captain Bishop coming up the gulch, with a **huge** torch-light on his shoulders. He looks like a fiend waving brands and lighting the fires of hell, and the men in the opposite gulch are imps lighting delusive fires in inaccessible crevices, over yawning chasms. At last we meet Captain Bishop with his flaming torch" (n. 65). And so the brilliant description continues.

What is all this but the **chuh yuen** of the ancient record? Here surely is "an illumination of torches."

Torches and Climbing, say the Ancients.

Torches and Climbing, say the Moderns.

We can readily understand why the ancient occupants of the stone houses in the Grand Canyon, should have used the torches so liberally and conveniently supplied by nature throughout the region where their light is too often sadly or desperately needed. We have been informed by a modern visitor that ruined cave habitations are to be seen along "lofty and inaccessible ledges." And these dwellings "were reached by very narrow, precipitous, and devious paths, and being extremely difficult to attain by the occupants themselves, presented an impregnable front to invaders."

Surely here torches would often come in handy.

Dr. Fewkes believes that the ancient occupants of the cliff or cave houses chose hazardous sites in order to be out of the reach of enemies. He says: [Pg 27]

"The pressure of outside tribes, or what may be called human environment, probably had much to do originally with the choice of caves for houses. The experienced archaeologist also draws attention to Jackson's remark that finger imprints answering to those of women, "may still be traced in the mortar" of the dwellings (n. 66). Many interiors indeed are covered with smooth plaster in which the impressions of small and delicate fingers appear.

Of course, women and children formerly lived on the "inaccessible ledges"; and sons, fathers, husbands, or brothers, away perhaps hunting in distant glens or forests, were comparatively free from anxiety concerning the condition of loved ones at home. And if savages with tomahawks and scalping knives came stealing through ravines to the foot of impregnable stairways, the mothers aloft, pressing children to their breasts and looking down on baffled foes, must have felt something of the emotion which throbs through the well-known lines, written indeed by a woman,—
For the strength of the hills we bless Thee,
  Our God, our fathers' God!
Thou hast made Thy children mighty
  By the touch of the mountain sod;
Thou hast fixed our ark of refuge
  Where the spoiler's foot ne'er trod;—
For the strength of the hills we bless Thee,
  Our God, our fathers' God!
And if in the darkness of night, the awaited signal or cry were heard arising

from the heart of the abyss, how quickly the doors would be opened and ropes lowered and torches lighted to help the hunters to their homes on high! Torches flaming and eyes gleaming. Lights flashing in all directions. An illumination of torches. No wonder the Canyon was noted for its **chuh yuen** and cave dwellings.

Lights, Climbing, and Caves, say the Ancients.

Lights, Climbing, and Caves, say the Moderns.

The account continues thus:

26. **Leang** (the principal, the chief; a bridge, a beam.)

27. **kien** (official writing; to mark; a slip of bamboo for making notes on; a classifier of folios or sheets.)

28. **wan** (strokes, lines, literature, literary; a despatch.)

29. **Ta** (Great.)

30. **Hoh** (Canyon.)

31. **fu** (to spread abroad as decrees; to exact; to demand.)

A **leang** or chief is here referred to in connection with the Great Canyon. The ruler is not exactly called the King or supreme head (**chwen suh**). Indeed, we have been already informed that the head ruler was a mere nurseling (at the time when he abandoned his Lute in the Canyon) and such an infant carried about by the mother who had just brought him into the world, among the cliffs and canyons, would evidently have been unable to either write or issue decrees. Of course, however, a nominally subordinate chief (or [Pg 28] **leang**) might have attended to the details of government and ruled or directed the movements of the Sun people in the name of the infant King. Such a minister might have spread abroad decrees or commands within the Canyon.

Are any writings to be seen on its walls?

An explorer already in part quoted, says: "At last we meet Captain Bishop with his flaming torch. On a broad shelf we find the ruins of an old stone house, the walls of which are broken down, and we can see where the ancient people who lived here—a race more highly civilized than the present—had made a gar-

den, and used a great spring, that comes out of the rocks, for irrigation. On some rocks near by we discover some curious etchings" (n. 67).

Here are cliff writings.

Again, on the brink of a rock 200 feet high stands an old house. Its walls are of stone, laid in mortar, with much regularity. On the face of the cliff, under the building and along down the river for 200 or 300 yards, there are many etchings."

Here are writings "spread abroad" within the **Ta-hoh** or Great Canyon. Not painted on the cliffs, but cut into the stone! Beyond the reach or malice of savage tribes, they doubtless furnished directions to friendly clans, telling where certain companies had moved, and so forth.

"On many of the tributaries of the Colorado I have heretofore examined their deserted dwellings. Sometimes the mouths of caves have been walled across and there are many other evidences to show their anxiety to secure defensible positions. Probably the nomadic tribes were sweeping down upon them, and they resorted to these cliffs and canyons for safety. Here I stand where these now lost people stood centuries ago, and look over this strange country."

The former chief of the Ethnological Bureau also says that at the mouth of the Colorado Chiquito he discovered some curious remains, such as ruins and pottery, also "etchings and hieroglyphics on the rocks."

Some of the cliff or cave dwellings are singularly impressive. Baron Nordenskiold, says of one, called the "Cliff Palace," that it well deserves its proud name, "for with its round towers and high walls . deep in the mysterious twilight of the cavern, and defying in their sheltered site the ravages of time, it resembled at a distance an enchanted castle."

And Chapin exclaims: "Surely its discoverer had not overstated the beauty and magnitude of this strange ruin. There it was, occupying a great oval space under a grand cliff wonderful to behold, appearing like an immense ruined castle with dismantled towers" (n. 68).

And yet Dr. Fewkes very rationally refuses to regard it as a "palace"—occupied merely by a king and servants or else officers of state managing an empire. Of course some nook within sheltered its ruler. But it is merely a pueblo—set within a cave. One French visitor says: "Il est probable que Cliff-Palace n'abritait pas moins de 500 personnes" (n. 69).

At this rate it would have required forty such structures (or equivalent clusters of apartments) to shelter, say, 20,000 individuals. [Pg 29]

There is mention of cave dwellings in connection with the Great Canyon; and as Sun people with a supreme ruler (although but a suckling) are represented as climbing within the chasm, with the aid of torches, we expect to find curious remains in connection with the caverns. Nor are we disappointed. Here are mouths of caves walled up for defensive purposes. Here are ramparts, towers, and fortified structures classed with castles.

We are informed that decrees were spread abroad in the Canyon; and searching for the ancient inscriptions, we find that they are cut into the cliffs. This shows that the former dwellers were able to cut and work stone; and abundant remains of masonry are at hand to sustain this deduction.

The personality of the **ju**, or suckling ruler, remains to be investigated, and should yield curious—most surprising—results; but, of course, reasonable, logical critics will not for an instant confound such an inquiry with that just finished. Even absolute failure to unearth the facts with regard to the Prince and his royal mother, can not shake the plain fact that we have actually found an account of the Grand Canyon, the Colorado River, and the Gulf of California, in an ancient Chinese book.

## PIMO AND THE CASAS GRANDES

It may further be remarked that the Chinese paragraph which immediately follows the account of our Canyon, mentions a place called "Pi-mo."

This is its pronunciation in Canton, but in Shanghai, where **mo** is accorded the sound of **mu** (see Williams' dict. p. 1154 and p. 1186, column 6) **Pi-mo** would be called **Pi-mu**. Now, this Pi-mo or Pi-mu is said (see existing translation) to be situated in the "south-east corner of the desert beyond the eastern sea."

Proceeding eastward until the "Eastern Sea," which washes the coast of China, is crossed, the modern investigator reaches California and Arizona. And here, in the region or basin of the Colorado, he finds a place still called "Pi-mo." It is in Arizona, with a "desert" of sand—the desert of California and Sonora—to its west and south, and a region of running streams, grass, and forests to its east. **Pimo** is itself in the "desert"—in a "south-east corner of the desert beyond the Eastern Sea." It is entirely dependent on artificial irrigation for its limited power to support human beings.

Here are ruined buildings whose origin is shrouded in mystery and around or about which controversies have raged for centuries.

One visitor, an American officer, states that his General "asked a Pimo, who made the house I had seen?" The house was one of the Casas Grandes in the neighborhood of Pimo. Who had made it? was now the question. The reply was: "It was built by the son of the most beautiful woman who once dwelt in yon mountain; she was fair and all the handsome men came to court her, but in vain; when they came, they paid tribute, and out of this small store she fed all people in times of famine and it did not diminish."

Moreover, "at last she brought forth a boy, who was the builder of all these houses." [Pg 30]

The Pimo Indian "seemed unwilling to talk about them, but said there were plenty more of them to the north, south, west, etc." (note 70.)

[Was the royal suckling or Prince ever carried down into the neighboring Grand Canyon by the beneficent being, his mother? Was he a **shao hao** (as the Chinese might say) or little Child of the Sun? Did he ever see the Cliff Palace? Were he and his people connected with the cave and cliff-dwellings? And when he retired from the Canyon did he fail to take with him a Lute?]

If the royal suckling (or **ju**) of the Chinese account ever actually lived in the neighborhood of the Grand Canyon, or in the vicinity of Pimo, and was connected with a restless or troubled nation of Cliff Dwellers or stone-house builders, why should not the Indians have some traditional, even if but hazy recollection of both the suckling and his imperial mother? The forefathers of the Pimos must have beheld them, and it is difficult to suppose that the ancient legendary knowledge has completely evaporated from the aboriginal memory. As we have learned the construction of the Casas Grandes at Pimo is connected with the advent or movements of an intelligent, even if harassed race of Builders who owed allegiance to a Princess or her child. And if it is a fact that in a time of famine the royal lady fed the ancestors of the Pimos, we wonder not that the nation has enshrined her image within its ceaseless, throbbing heart. The hill-top on which she gave birth to her suckling is remembered to the present hour and was pointed to by the Pimo interpreter when telling the American General about the merciful being who fed the hungry in a time of famine (and perhaps had relieved or cheered his own ancestor.)

Let us not overlook or snub the fact that Pimo—the Pimo of "the region beyond the Eastern Sea" is actually mentioned in the same breath with the Grand Canyon and the Gulf. It is represented by characters numbered 9 and 10 in the extract from the ancient Chinese volume, now set before the patient and intelligent reader who appreciates or perceives the difficulties connected with the present investigation.

The last column (reading from right to left) consists of 12 characters, which express the following sense: Ta—**Hg**—east—south—corner—**has**—**shan** (mountain or height)—called—**Pi mo**—**ti**—**kiu**.

The 11th term, **ti**, stands for "place;" and a **kiu** is a level-topped hill. As it is also called a **shan** (see No. 7), the **kiu** should be a prominent eminence having a level space on top.

The name **Pi-mo** is expressed by putting **Pi**, which signifies "skin" or "case," along with **mo**, which simply stands for "mother."

A mother, or a maternal case is connected with the **Pi-mo kiu** or level-topped hill. Is such an eminence to be seen in the vicinity of Pi-mo? Has it a flat summit? Are there any signs that it was inhabited by the queen of the Builders? The Pimo Indian told the general that on the hill-top in the vicinity—in the Lower Gila Valley—a female ruler gave birth to a child. Is there any foundation for the legend? Where is her house?

Referring to the structures in Arizona, an observer draws particular attention to one "comparatively intact in the lower Gila valley." He says: "The [Pg 31] hill on which it is built rises abruptly from the surrounding lowlands to the height of a full thousand feet. Near the northwest corner the ancient strategists began at a height of thirty feet, carving a narrow pathway to the summit. Here an irregular stone staircase has been made, passable by one person at a time. At intervals watchtowers were constructed, from which huge boulders could be hurled down upon the advancing foe.

[Pg 32] "The road makes three complete circles above the hill before reaching the upper **level**." [Here is a **level**-topped hill or **kiu**.] "Here another monument of early fortitude inspired by the love of life presents itself. There is, perhaps, three acres of **level** rock on the summit. For a depth of nearly two feet the entire **plateau** is covered with rich soil 'packed up' from below. When one pauses to think of the immense labor involved in carrying this mass of earth up the irregular winding stone staircase, a feeling of admiration springs up for these simple patient people."

It is plain that there is a **level**-topped hill (or **kiu**) in the vicinity of Pimo. And it is directly connected in Indian tradi-

tion with the movements of a race of builders who reared "all these houses," and were directed or governed by a beneficient being who here gave birth to a remarkable prince. But it is enough at present to observe that the Chinese symbols connect Pimo—the Pimo of the "region beyond the Eastern Sea"—with a Mother, or notable Birth. And when the American General—in our region beyond the Eastern Sea—inquires at Pimo for information, concerning its now silent and forsaken ruins, the Pimo interpreter instantly responds by raising his arm and pointing to the hill of the royal birth.

The Hill of the Maternal Case is there, say the Chinese.

The Hill of the Maternal Case is Here, say the Pimos.

The hill is prominent or lofty and quite level on top. It is in truth a **kiu**

(pronounced like our own word cue) and holds aloft some impregnable dwellings and also a green spot or abandoned garden—clay having been carried aloft a thousand feet by devoted Builders in part to raise flowers for the young mother. But, of course, her own bud was the brightest of all. And every one told her so. And what a wide view from the summit! And how cool the air up there! How different from the blazing Canyon (with its hidden or abandoned Lute.)

"The General asked a Pimo, who made the house I had seen? 'It is the Casa de Montezuma', said he; it was built by the son of the most beautiful woman who once dwelt in yon mountain; she was fair—"

Notice here the name "Montezuma."

The Casas Grandes at Pimo were fortunately seen by Spanish explorers in the 16th century, and "the Indians then assigned them an age of no less than 500 years." (note 71.)

Of course the Casa Grande Montezuma (or Builder Prince of the 11th century) could not have been the Montezuma who was overthrown by Cortez in the 16th century. As well confound William of Normandy with William of Holland, because each was a William! Let fools do that! [Pg 33]

One writer says with regard to the legends of the sedentary Indians, that "the name of Montezuma runs through all of these—not generally referring to the king whom we are accustomed to identify with that name, but to the great chief of the golden or heroic age." (n. 72)

There are noticeable variations in the name or title of the ancient king. Thus one Spanish explorer speaks of "the Casa Grande, or palace of **Moc**-te-zu-ma" (n. 73.)

Here we have **Moc** (or **Mok**, as it is by others spelled) instead of **Mon** (ti-zuma.)

Another authority furnishes the spelling **Mo**-te-cuh-**zoma**, and adds, that it is "found written also **Moc**-te-zu-ma, Mu-teczuma, Mo-texuma" (n. 74.)

Notice the three different spellings or sounds—**Mo**, **Mu**, and **Mok**, prefixed to "**te-zuma**."

The title **te** or **ti** (or **te-cuh**) signifies warrior or lordly ruler (n. 75.) As for **suma** it is said to mean "sad, angry, or severe." [But soma may include an allusion to the water of immortality and embrace the notion of divine descent.]

**Mok** (the **te-zuma**) **Mo** or **Mu** were names or titles bestowed on the 11th century Builder Prince who was connected with the construction of the Casas Grandes in the Pimo section, and was born on a prominent hill-top there. He was **Mok**, **Mo** or **Mu**.

Turning to the Chinese account we find that the royal **ju** or suckling connected with the region of the Grand Canyon and Pimo, was likewise known as **Mu**. (note 76.)

In addition, the suckling is repeatedly called a **ti** (or **te** as it is just as often spelled.) And this, so far, agrees with the title of the Pimo infant, whose name is frequently said to be **Mu-ti** (zuma.)

A **Mu-ti**, say the Chinese.

A **Mu-ti**, say the Pimos.

According to the Chinese record, the imperial (**ti** or **te**) heir apparent (or **yuen-tsz**) suckling or baby (**ju**) whose estate or patrimony (**chan**) was **Loh-ming** (name of a region) lived or resided (**ku**) as the tender, delicate youth (**yao**) **Mu**.

Here we see that the heir apparent the ju or baby was both **Mu** and a **ti**. The old account connects the infantile ruler with a region called Loh-ming. We need not delay to ascertain the position of this province or land; enough now to observe that wherever it was, the **ju** and **ti** lived there (or lived some where) as the pleasing and tender **Mu**.

The baby was **Mu**.

This name, like some of our own names, such as Grace, Patience, Clement, is frequently used as an adjective. It may stand for either "beauty" or "majesty," but it is also, at times, a surname. (note 77.) [Pg 34]

As already seen, the Great Canyon with the connected bottomless abyss, in the region beyond the Eastern Sea, is connected with the Sun and Moon Shan. And on this Shan is "the Great Men's Country" (see existing translation.)

Now a Chinese comment (note 78) informs us that the **forts** of the entirely great **Mu** formerly held or possessed this Great Men's Country (which is on the Sun and Moon Shan.)

Information is next furnished concerning the largest Walrusses, and it is plain that the polar region is referred to. The account is quite clear, as any Chinese scholar can see, now that we have pointed out the position of the passage.

It might seem advisable to prove that the haunt of the Walrus was known to the ancient Chinese writers who have furnished accounts of America, but it is unnecessary to do this, seeing that the phenomenon of Ten Suns, which is only visible at the Arctic Circle, is referred to in the ancient books. Moreover, as we have learned, appearances of five or seven suns (or moons) shining simultaneously in the sky, are distinctly connected with the Sun and Moon Shan. It was therefore known that the mountain system of North America, stretches upward—like the Branches of a Tree—from the vicinity of the Grand Canyon to the Polar region, or place of the Ten Suns. And from a point here, the shores of North-eastern Tartary or Asia can be seen without even the aid of an opera-glass.

It now appears that in the remote past there was a ruler named **Mu** dwelling in the mountainous land which stretches from the Grand Canyon to the Arctic Ocean. His domain was on the Sun and Moon Shan.

And he had fortified dwellings or forts.

Where, today, are the remains of the ancient strongholds?

One observer says with reference to the cliff-dwellings, that they "have the appearance of fortified retreats. The occupants, on account of "decending hordes devised these **unassailable** retreats. The builders hold no smallest niche in recorded history. Their aspirations, their struggles and their fate are all unwritten, save in these crumbling stones, which are their sole monuments and meagre epitaph. Here once they dwelt. They left no other print on time." (note 79.)

The "unassailable retreats" noticed by this melancholy writer may well be some of the strongholds of Mu and his followers or warriors. The ancient pueblos (or Casas Grandes) are of great strength. When the "ladders are drawn in, the various sides present a perpendicular front to an enemy, and the building itself becomes a **fortress**." Further, "The strength of the walls of these structures was proved during the Mexican war, when it was found that they were impregnable to field-artillery." (note 80. )

The Spanish soldier, Castenada, in the 16th century said with regard to the Pimo Casa Grande, that "it seemed to have served as a fortress." (note 81.)

Now, **Pimo**—represented by the symbols for a maternal case and hill—is mentioned on the very page of the Chinese book which notices our Grand Canyon. Then, we are told that cliff-dwellings were here and a Sun Prince [Pg 35] (at first a mere **ju** or infant) called **Mu**, and that he or his followers erected forts or fortresses.

And here we find no scarcity of ancient strongholds.

And when we ask the Indians for the name of the ruler who governed the now decaying strongholds, their answer is—**Mu**.

The very title in the Chinese book.

**Mu**, say the Ancients.

**Mu**, say our Indians.

It may be said that some of the latter pronounce the title **Mo**. One of our philologists speaks of "Montezuma, or more correctly, **Mo**tecuhzoma." (note 82.)

Another authority says: "Montezuma, or more correctly, **Moc**tezuma." (note 83.)

In his account of the Casa Grande, the old time Spanish traveler, Padre Garces, says: On this river is situated the house which they call **Moc**tezuma's. (note 84.)

It is evident that the two pronunciations **Mo** and **Mok** are preferred to **Mon** (tezuma) and that **Mu** has also its advocates.

Curiously enough, these three sounds **Mu**, **Mo**, and **Mok**, are likewise applied to the one character by the Chinese literati.

The identical symbol which Williams calls **Mu** is in another dictionary (see Bailley's, iii, p. 246) termed **Mo**.

Morrison (vol. IV, p. 600-1) says that the two sounds **Mu** and **Mo** are both applied, and that in Canton this selfsame character is called **Mok**.

It thus appears that the builder or ruler of the fortresses in the region beyond the Eastern Sea, might be called **Mu**, **Mo**, or **Mok**.

And in the region referred to—"the region beyond the Eastern Sea"—we find many strongholds or forts (as well as cave-dwellings;) and when antiquarians inquire of the Indians for the name of the ancient Builder Prince, they are variously informed that he was the glorious **Mu**, **Mo**, or **Mok**.

If the royal infant (or **ju**) became in process of time a ruler of fortresses (**tai**) which "formerly held the Great Men's Country" (on the Sun and Moon Shan) would be surprising to find that he himself had been born within the shelter of a **tai** or fortress? And what is the fortified hill at Pimo but a fortress? He counts it as the first of the forts of **Mu** or **Mo-ti** in "the region beyond the Eastern Sea."

Remember that our own government has erected numbers of forts on hilltops throughout the South-west expressly for the purpose of holding such tribes as the Navajoes and Apaches in check. (And in addition we are furnishing the red men with supplies.) But in the 11th century there were no Congressional appropriations, no detachments of troops hurrying down from Washington to preserve order. Yet the ancestors of our savage tribes were certainly there. And although the warrior chieftans immediately around the young queen appear to have been filled with jealousy of each other, it is certain that they [Pg 36] were united as one in devising for the princess a calm or sure retreat which no barbaric host could take by assault. From its base the savage ranks would reel, or break into foam like waves of the sea.

Aloft in this secure retreat she gave birth to **Mo**.

Who was his father?

The American General already referred to, supplies his own report of the Pimo interpreter's words:

"All he knew was a tradition amongst them, 'that in bygone days, a woman of surpassing beauty resided in a green spot in the mountains near the place where we were encamped. All the men admired and paid court to her. She received the tributes of their devotion, grain, skins, etc., but gave no love or other favor in return. Her virtue and her determination to remain unmarried were equally firm. There came a drought which threatened the world with famine. In their distress, people applied to her, and she gave corn from her stock, and the supply seemed to be endless. Her goodness was unbounded. One day, as she was lying asleep with her body exposed, a drop of rain fell on her stomach, which produced conception. A son was the issue, the founder of a new race which built all these houses'. The houses of the people (the agricultural or sedentary Pimos) are mere sheds, thatched with willow and corn stalks" (n. 85.)

This report is more rational than the other in so far as it represents the multitudinous houses of stone or adobe as being reared by a "race" rather than by a "boy"! But, of course, the "son" could not have been the "founder" of his mother or of her ancestors. It is further apparent that the infant could not have been either the builder or inventor of the house or stronghold in which he was born.

Of course it is an impossibility to get at the exact truth in relation to the mysterious birth. The unwedded lady's own account ought to constitute a sufficient explanation, and would—but for the unfortunate historic fact that no mother has ever been known to tell her children the truth about their production. Even Christian mothers lie precisely like Pagans in this respect, and are just as thorough-going humbugs as Hannah in the temple, when questioned for details. They will tell a poor helpless, green, inquiring child, for instance, that they

found him in a cabbage, when the actual truth is that they got him from a stork. We therefore unanimously dismiss their worse than useless testimony as that of a shameless pack of preposterous deluders.

It is probable that the Pimo princess may have been secretly wedded or united to some man whom she really loved and preferred to all others. Yet an open avowal of such preference might have caused his death or might have turned the love of rival suitors into hate and brought about the ruin of the already sufficiently perplexed and troubled nation.

But would not the birth of the infant have revealed all?

Certainly, but in the present instance the Queen seems to have contented herself with the announcement that she had got her child from Heaven. Her friends, including doubtless the priests, at once spread abroad the story that the infant—the Child of the Sun—was of celestial origin. This tale may not have [Pg 37] completely satisfied the numerous rival claimants for the lady's hand. But how disprove it? And why assail or shake the authority of the beautiful young queen? Why not draw closer together, bury their mutual animosities or rivalries and face the murderous hordes thronging the passes of the Rocky Mountains and slopes of the Mississippi Valley? Why not grasp at the hope—embodied in the suckling born on the hilltop—that Heaven had furnished a leader, a reincarnated divinity of the wandering nation, who would guide the despairing people onward to new fields of national glory and prosperity.

It may of course be said that such predictions were never realized, but it is certain that they were cherished. Even the Mokis, Tunis and Pimos still regard **Mo-ti** as immortal and await his return. He is "the demigod of their earliest traditions, watching over them from Heaven and waiting to come again to bring to them victory and a period of millenial glory and happiness" (n. 86.) And, of course, those who actually followed the leader **Mu** must have felt strongly the ties of affection and veneration. And who were the people who got across to Mongolia with accounts of our Grand Canyon, Gulf and Continental Tree—crowned with its wreath of multiplied suns?

[Doubtless the notion that our **Mu-te** (or **Te-Mu**) was of divine origin, had a surprising, stimulating effect. Curiously enough, Asiatic writers notice a **Te-mu** (**Te-mu-dzin** or **Temugin**) who arose in Tartary in the early part of the 12th century, and therefore might be regarded as the contemporary of our **Mu** born at Pimo about the year 1100. Some say this Tartarean conqueror was called Timour or Temur-chi, and his origin is wrapt in mystery. One account treats him as a demigod, but other statements assume that a divinity was his remote ancestor. He is said to belong to the race that broke out of Irkena Kon (or the mountain valley), situated in some out of the way and dangerous region. Personally this **Mu** came from a distant land. Some historians whose time is valuable readily find Irkena Kon in the vicinity of the Caspian Sea, but others declare that it must be situated in the direction of the Arctic Ocean!

[In his old age, in or about the year 1153, this supposed demigod had a child born to him. The name of Temudzin or Temugin was bestowed upon the infant. When thirteen years old his father—the demigod—died, and the extensive empire which the parent had established fell into political pieces. Gibbon, in his "Decline and Fall of the Roman Empire," chap. LXIV, says that the young prince Temugin could only claim authority over about 12,000 families. We should never overlook this fact when contemplating his career. Every incident in his history is known. His name has resounded through the world. He rose to be a mighty conqueror. He became Jenghiz Khan—King of Kings—grandsire of Kublai Khan, ancestor of Tamerlane and the Great Moguls, and of no end of Persian or Moslem Sultans or Kings.

[The immediate followers of Jenghiz Khan always declared that success awaited him because he was the son of a God. Petis de la Croix denounces such

a claim as a piece of "insolence," yet it might better be regarded as a form of delusion. But notice the victorious lengths to which this delusion carried believers. And the notion promulgated at Pimo, in the midst of crowd [Pg 38]ing calamities,—that the royal infant was a Son of Heaven,—might have been intended to console and stimulate a despairing nation. And the spiritual stimulus appears to have transported its believers to such lengths that aboriginal Americans seem to have lost track of the demigod, and know not from what point he may return.

[The father of Temugin was the founder of the **Yuen** dynasty, or at all events an ancestral king. He is generally called Yisukai or Pysukai Behadur, but such is a mere title, signifying "9th hero," and not a proper name at all. Some lucid commentators will positively tell us that it was not the father of Jenghiz Khan, but his 9th father or ancestor, who was the God. But with such hair-splitting we need not concern ourselves. Enough to note the uplifting, psychological effect or result of faith or belief in divine aid or protection. No wonder David exclaims: "Thy rod and Thy staff, they comfort me."

[In the case of the Tartars, the results of their exalted faith were indeed surprising. The Crusades of the Christians had proved a failure. Jerusalem had passed from their hands. Richard, King of England, had been taken prisoner. The Moslems, according to Gibbon, were preparing for the invasion of Europe. Their brethren were actually intrenched in the heart of Spain. Enraged against western nations for the long war waged against their power, armies were gathering for the conquest and plunder of Christendom. The crescent instead of the cross, says Gibbon, was to glitter on the spire of St. Paul's.

[But at this very juncture, Jenghiz Khan and his followers came pouring forth from the wilds of Tartary. The Sultan felt secure within his line of fortified cities which hitherto had repelled every assault. But the Tartarean host—led by warriors of the race from Irkena Kon—overthrew the Moslems in every

encounter. They ransacked the provinces and gave the cities to the flames. And the children or successors of the conqueror completed the work which he had begun. Bagdad which for ages had successfully defied the invading, crusading armies of Europe, was destroyed, and an end put to the Caliphate so long enthroned within its historic walls. The conquest of China was completed by Kublai Khan, and an empire formed which stretched from the Indian Ocean to the Arctic, and from the Pacific to the Mediterranean Sea.]

Even traditions of tribes that most certainly remained behind in Arizona and consequently did not disappear in company with the mysterious **Mu** or Mo-te, declare that he was an agent of Providence. He was the "equal" of the "Great Spirit" and "was often considered identical with the Sun" (n. 87.) Had he remained in Arizona, his son in due time might have claimed divine descent through his father the demigod.

## CHINESE KNOWLEDGE OF THE PIMO DEMIGOD.

But if the **Mu-te** (or **Te-Mu**,) builder or ruler of fortresses in the region of Pimo and the Grand Canyon, was identical with our Pimo **Mu-te**, he should be referred to as semi-divine, in the Chinese record.

And so he actually is. Even here the evidence does not fail. But conception of the little sun-child did not occur on the well watched or guarded [Pg 39] hilltop at Pimo. It was in a green wilderness noted for its hay or grass and butchering of beasts, that a phantasm approached the female—and so on.

Fortunately we can turn away from this particular account of the visit of incubus, seeing that the necessary information is more conveniently furnished elsewhere (n. 88.) The name of a mountain, which may or may not have been far indeed from the Grand Canyon, is furnished, and we are informed that **Shao Hao** dwelt (**ku**) there (**chi**.) In addition he is called a sovereign (**ti** or **te**) and a **shan**.

Now this term, **shan**, according to Williams (p. 737,) stands for "the gods, the divinities, a god, a supernatural good being; divine; spiritual, as being higher than man; godlike, wonderful, superhuman; to deify.

The **Shao Hao** (or **Mu-ti**) is a **shan** or god.

A god! say the Chinese.

A god! say the Indians.

Taking the account as it stands, it appears that an incarnated god (in the shape of the **Shao Hao Mu**) was at one time within the Grand Canyon (which still retains his "lute.")

Notice that the "country contiguous to the mighty chasm is called the "Shao Hao's country."

Next observe that the vast chasm (or **ta-hoh**) is itself called the Great Canyon of the Incarnated God (or **Keang Shang**.) **Shang** stands for "Heaven" or supreme;" and Keang signifies "to descend from a higher level, to come from the sky, to fall as rain, to come into the world as Christ did" (Williams.) The contiguous country is named in honor of the **Shao Hao**, or sun-child, who is called a **shan** or god. And "**Keang Shang's** ta-hoh" or great Canyon is also named in honor of this **shan** or god— this incarnated god.

And here, "in the region beyond the Eastern Sea," the land is ringing with his name. He was **Mu** or **Mo-te** and a builder of forts, and above and beyond all this he was an incarnation of the Great Spirit!

"The name, at this moment, is as familiar to every Indian, Apache and Navajoe as that of our Savior or Washington is to us" (n. 89.)

Bancroft says: "Under restrictions, we may fairly regard him as the Melchizedek, the **Moses**, and the Messiah of the Pueblo desert-wanderers from an Egypt that history is ignorant of, and whose name even tradition whispers not."

A Messiah and Demigod! say the Chinese.

A Messiah and Demigod! say Americans.

Bancroft, says, that according to Indian paintings or traditions, the Messiah or Demigod of Pueblo tradition had red or yellow hair.

Then Mo was a white man and his mother a white woman.

Such a conclusion agrees completely with the teaching of the ancient Chinese book just quoted. We are informed with reference to a certain mountain, that: **Ki** (the) **shan** (god or spirit) **poh** (white) **ti** (sovereign) **Shao hao** (little sun-child) **ku** (dwelt) **chi** (there).

Next appears a comment stating in the plainest possible terms that **Shao Hao** of the **Kin Tien** dynasty was a virtuous or excellent ruler. [Pg 40]

The **Shao Hao** who was at the Tahoh or Great Canyon is here called a **White King**.

Mons. Rosny, in his French translation, declares that the divine or superhuman **Shao Hao** was "l'empereur Blanc. " (note 90.)

One well known writer and archaeologist says with reference to the builders of some structures in the Pimo region, that there is "reason to suppose that they were a light-skinned people. At least one red-haired skull and one with still lighter hair were found. Hair has been but rarely found not over a half dozen times in all. In three cases it was black." (note 91.)

According to aboriginal testimony, 800 years have rolled by since the time of burial, and hair has lingered on but few of the heads it once adorned. But when discovered it is seen to be quite different from the hair of the Indians.

Those interested in the subject of the Cliff-dwellers should study the accurate reports of the Ethnological Bureau and also the writings of Editor Peet the well known "American Antiquarian." These works should be in the libraries of all Americanists.

According to the American Antiquarian, Doctor Birdsall reports that dried bodies have been found in tombs on the Mesa Verde in Arizona and the "hair of the head has been found partly preserved on some mummies. It is said to be of fine texture, not coarse like Indian hair and varying in color from shades of yellowish brown to reddish brown and black" . The Wetherills exhumed one mummy having a short brownish beard. " (note 92.)

We are further informed that mummies have been taken from "a hermetically sealed cave in the Canyon of the Gila River," and two of the bodies were those of women. The females "retain their long, flowing silken hair." The "bodies were covered with highly colored clothes, which crumbled on exposure. Three kinds were saved, and one a deep blue woven in diamond shapes. No implements or utensils were found. All the consuls and many scientific men inspected the mummies yesterday. Among those present were Henry A. Ward, of Rochester, N. Y., Kate Field, Dr. Harkness, Academy of Sciences." Other Doctors and Professors were present and also "Historian Bancroft." (n. 93.)

In addition to all this, Professor C. L. Webster, the accomplished, painstaking, and trusted scientist of Charles City, Iowa, has unearthed a body whose silent testimony is truly inestimable. In the "Archaeological Bulletin," issued by the International Society of Archaeologists (Madison, Indiana,) for July and September, 1912, we find a photograph of a mummy brought to light by the Professor in a cliff-house on a head stream of the Gila.

The body is that of a child, and its preservation is due to "the chemical elements of the soil," etc.

"The hair on the head of the mummy was of a beautiful dark brown color, and of a soft and silky texture," and "the hair on the head of this mummified child is of the same color and texture (only finer) as that of adults found braided in long plaits in an adjoining room"—Page 78.

The Professor believes that "different races" were here contending for the mastery of the region, and that "one or more of them were driven out (perhaps destroyed) suddenly" (see article 1.) [Pg 41]

Another archaeologist says, that "quite recently hieroglyphics were discovered in the Tonto Basin country, depicting the driving out of white people by red men, and local archaeologists have set up a theory that the people who once cultivated these valleys were white. The present Indians have many legends of white men being in their country before the advent of the Spanish conquistodores. Father Marcas Niza, a pious Jesuit, who accompanied Coronado on his march through this section in search of the seven lost cities of Cibola, speaks frequently of allusions made by Indians to white bearded men who were here before" (n. 94.)

[In tracking the missing white race, remember that some of the Toltecs, like the Mayas of Yucatan, compressed the skull in childhood, that they had among them a sprinkling of very large men (quinames,) and that in the wilderness their mode of living would be more like that of Indians than of cultured, civilized people.]

Mons. Charney has argued that the Mexican Toltecs were of a white race, but very foolishly argues (like Baron Humboldt) that the Toltecs marched from Mongolia to Mexico in the 6th century. The illustrious Humboldt has served Archaeology enormously by drawing attention to the absolute and startling identity of the Zodiacal signs of the Manchu Tartars with those of Central America (see Mr. Vining's exceedingly comprehensive and valuable work entitled "An Inglorious Columbus.")

Skilled, scientific archaeologists connected with the Washington Bureau have all along been contending that the cliff or cave dwellings, forts, pueblos, and mounds of North America were constructed by native-born Americans, rather than by Toltecs moving in, say, the 6th century from Tartary to Arizona or Mexico.

Therefore, as the Toltecs (sun-people and architects or builders) were certainly settled in Mexico for some centuries prior to the 11th (when the remnant disappeared,) the ancestors of the pale-faced and cultured people (see Vining's chapter on the "Toltecs") may like ourselves have reached America by crossing the Atlantic. The Greek face, the Celtic face, the Saxon face, and the Jewish or Semitic face are all seen carved on the tottering walls of temples and palaces in Yucatan (see Charney's es-

says.)

Moving to the Vale of Mexico, the Toltecs tried with more or less success to keep on neighborly terms with the red skinned people. But thoughtless propagation produced more mouths than could be filled—except with human flesh. Open war broke out in the 11th century. The Aztecs or others of the red tribes almost annihilated the Whites; and Topiltzin Quetzalcoatl, the "last" King of the Toltecs fled north from Chapultepec,—the selfsame Chapultepec which in our own day has seen the downfall of Maxmillian and the flight of Diaz.

May not the fair and beautiful Princess at Pimo have belonged to the outcast Mexican royal family? May not her idolized child have inherited titles absurdly out of place among the deserts of Arizona? And may not all the elements in our later Yankee nation have been represented in the pale-faced people that found refuge among the canyons and cliffs of the Colorado? If so, their remote or ancestral fathers and mothers were likewise no less our own. [Pg 42]

The curtain of history rises and shows the young Queen of the Builders on a hill top at Pimo. The structures there, according to aboriginal testimony were reared about the year 1100,—the very time when the Toltecs disappeared from the Vale of Mexico. And now the ruins are yielding up forms of the females who once tenanted those cliffs and contrived to get plaster and paint with which to adorn the now desolate and trembling walls. And the yellow, brown, or silky black hair on the heads of those women who sought to make their bleak and dreary homes attractive, shows unfailingly their race. Even an ostrich might see it!

Mons. Charney declares that the Toltecs expelled from Mexico in the 11th century were scholars, artists, astronomers, and philosophers. And their sisters were certainly no less cultured and refined.

Now, the Shan Hai King states that in "the region beyond the Eastern Sea" there is (or was) a "Country of Refined

Gentlemen."

And Charney argues that "a gentle race were the Toltecs, preferring the arts to war."

Refined and Gentle—men, says Charney.

Refined Gentlemen, says the Shan Hai King.

Certain comments collected by Jin Chin Ngan, and unnoticed in Mr. Vining's translation (p. 657), connect the Refined Gentlemen with pyramids (**k'iu**) and even declare that their dwellings were on mounds (**ling**).

And Charney says: "Now, the first thing that we find at the houses of Tula is an example of a mode of building entirely new and curious. The prevailing tendency of the Toltec is to place his dwellings and his temples likewise upon eminences and pyramids."

They lived upon Mounds, says Charney.

They lived upon Mounds, says the Shan Hai King.

"They are very gentle, and do not quarrel. They have fragrant plants. They have a flowering-plant which produces blossoms in the morning that die in the evening.

The Chinese account calls this vegetable production the **Hwa** plant, and as **Hwa** stands for "glory" (see Williams' Chinese dict.) it is apparent that the "Morning Glory" is referred to.

Botanist Wood says: "This **glorious** plant is a **native** of Tropical America and now universally cultivated. It is also nearly naturalized with us." (in the United States.)

"The flowers are ephemeral. Beginning to open soon after midnight, they greet the Sun at his rising, arrayed in all their **glory**" (Hwa) "and before he reaches the meridian, fold their robes and perish. But their work is done, and their successors, already in bud, will renew the gorgeous display the following morning."—P. 182.

Such a flower might be held to symbolize the fleeting glory of the generations which had lived and died in Central America. It still climbs about the temples of the Sun, saluting its divinity with a smile, and then falling prostrate among the desolate and forsaken altars. It may often be seen twining its arms [Pg 43] around the monuments of a buried Past, or pressing its lips to the dust of the vanished race it so speedily follows.

It lives but a day, says the American botanist.

It lives but a day, says the Shan Hai King.

Surely the works in Arizona are worthy of the exiled Toltecs.

One of the ancient stone structures, on a northern feeder of the Gila, is so strong, commodious, and so impregnably planted that by universal consent it is called a Castle. And because the Indian tribes persist in ascribing its construction to **Mu** or **Mo-te** it is known as "Montezuma's Castle." The Ethnological Bureau has interested itself in the preservation of this impressive work of the so-called Cliff-dwellers, and our Government has taken charge of it as a "National Monument." And **Ari-zona** is named in honor of the **Ari** or "Maiden"—the legendary Queen of the Pimo **zona** or Pimo valley. The mother referred to in the ancient Chinese record is thus remembered in the title of a Yankee sister State.

Her idolized son is said to have governed Forts, and in the vicinity of the Castle we find a number of forts. Dr. Fewkes says: "The **forts** were built on the summits, . and it is an instructive fact in this connection that one rarely loses sight of one of these hill **forts** before another can be **seen**." An "approaching foe" could be discerned and "smoke signals" would warn field-workers "to retreat to the **forts** for protection."—28th Rept. Bur. Amer. Ethnol., p. 207. (Read also connected pages for information relating to the forts and their builders. The same or an allied people erected also houses in natural caves or excavated them in soft rock. "—P. 219. The latter—the excavated dwellings are noticed in Asiatic books and will be dealt with in next pamphlet—if such is ever written.)

We have found the "Forts" and also Pimo (or Pima as some pronounce the name) with its Princess and her child.

And have we not found the Gulf and Canyon referred to by the departed Ancients. Have we not found everything except perhaps the abandoned imperial Lute? And even it may yet be recovered. Let it be dug for at the Cliff of the Harp. Perhaps it may yet be resurrected—

"A Harp that in darkness and silence forsaken

Has slumbered while ages rolled slowly along,

Once more in its own native land may awaken

And pour from its chords all the raptures of song.

"Unhurt by the dampness that o'er it was stealing,

Its strings in full chorus, resounding sublime,

May 'rouse all the ardor of patriot feeling

And gain a bright wreath from the relics of time."

[Pg 44]

## APPENDIX

(Note 1) see Mr. Vining's "An Inglorious Columbus," p. 659. (2) **Jin-Chin Ngan's** comment in 14th Book of the Shan Hai King. (3) Kane's work. (4) Van Troil's "Iceland," 1, 643: Headley's "Island of Fire," p. 100. (5) Dr. Le Plongeon's "Queen Moo," xl, xlii, 175. (6) Vining, 182, 659, 666. (7) Vining; 182. (8) Vining, 659. (9) Vining, 659. (10) see index for essays collected by Mr. Vining. (11) see Chinese version of Shan Hai King, with Jin-chin-ngan's notes, (the latter being omitted in Mr. V.'s translation, p. 661. ) (12) see either the **Shan Hai King**, book 14, or the translation of same. (13) Vin. 661. (14) Mark Twain's "Roughing It," p. 101. (15) Lieut. Ives' Report, Pt. 1, p. 23. (16) Powell's Report. (17) Scribners' Mag. Nov. 1890. (18) R. R. Co.'s Handbook on "Colorado." (19) Powell's Report.

(Note 20) Stanton in Scribners' Mag. Nov. 1890. (21) Mr. F. A. Ober. (22) (compare Mr. Vining's translations with original Chinese statement.) (23) **Jin-Chin-ngan's** note (never hitherto trans-

lated into English.) (24) Dunraven's "Great Divide." (25) Vin. 647. (26) Powell's Report, 29, 35, 86. (27) Powell, 32, 71. (28) Vin. 532. (29) Stanton. (30) Mr. Clampitt's "Echoes from the Rocky Mts." 218. (31) Powell, p. 30. (32) "Glimpses of America" (Phila. 1894) p. 80. (33) Stanton. (34) "Glimpses." 78. (35) Powell, 16, 30. (36) Ives. Pt. I, 28; ii, p. 8. (37) Powell, 63, 86. (38) "Glimpses," 78. (39) Ives, 42.

(Note 40) **Ives'** Rept., Pt. I, p. 73. (41) F. A. Ober in Brooklyn **Times**, June 19, 1897. (42) Sitgreaves, 17. (43) Ives, 66. (44) Ives, III, 49. (45) Powell, 125. (46) "Glimpses of Amer." 78. (47) Glimpses," 83. (48) Powell, 55, 60, 70. (49) Dellenbaugh's "Canyon Voyage," 139. (50) Powell, 65, 76. (51) G. W. James's "Wonders of the Colorado Desert," 30. (52) Murphy's "Three Wonderlands," 137. (53) Powell, 35, 63, 86, 90. (54) Piexot's "Romantic California," 67, 144, 148. (55) Ives. 23. (56) Sacred Mysteries of the Mayas", 90. (57) "Glimpses of Amer." p. 82. (58) F. A. Ober in the Brooklyn **Times**, June 19, '97. (59) Appleton's "New Amer. Cyc." Article Colorado.

(Note 60) Sitgreaves' report, p. 17. (61) Ives, 107. (62) Sitgreaves, p. 18. (63) Dellenbaugh's "Canyon Voyage," 255. (64) Powell's Report. (65) Powell, 34, 35, 124, 125. (66) Smithson. Ethnol. "Bulletin," No. 51, p. 18. (67) Powell, 125. (68) Ethnological "Bulletin," No. 51, pp. 14, 15. (69) Bulletin, No. 51, p. 19. (70) Johnson's Journal in Emory's "Reconn. of N. Mex.," etc., 598-9. (71) Appletons' "New Am. Cyc." Article "Casas Grandes." (72) L. B. Prince's "New Mex.," p. 24. (73) Elliott Cones 'Comments on Garces' Diary, p. 94. (74) Encyc. Americana, vol. X. (75) Vining, 411. (76) see 28th character from last in note by Jin Chin Ngan preceding assertion in text that the Canyon has a beautiful mountain (Vining, 661. ) (77) Morrison, IV, p. 601. (78) **Jin Chin Ngan**. (79) Murphy's "Three Wonderlands," 152.

Note (80) Amer. Cyc. IV, p. 50. (81) Bancroft's "Native Races," IV, 620. (82) New Internat. Encyc. XIII. (83)

Penny Cyc. Article "Mexico," p. 163. (84) Bancroft's "Native Races." (85) Emory, p, 83. (86) Prince's N. Mex. 24. (87) Prince's N. M. 24-6. (88) The **Shan Hai King**, Book II, section III, 14th mountain. (89) Emory, 64. (90) Shan Hai King, p. 83. (91) Mr Spears in N. Y. **Sun**. Sept. 3, 1893. (92) **Amer. Antiquarian**, May, 1892. (93) N. Y. **World**, Oct. 1887. (94) N. Y. **Recorder**, Feb. 19, 1893.

**TRANSCRIBER'S NOTE:** All apparent printer's errors retained.

CPSIA information can be obtained at www.ICGtesting.com
Printed in the USA
BVOW07s1021040314

346623BV00008B/244/P